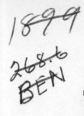

teaching techniques

GUIDING PRINCIPLES FOR CHURCH TEACHING

1974 REVISION

1899

EVANGELICAL TEACHER TRAINING ASSOCIATION

110 Bridge Street • Box 327 • Wheaton, Illinois 60187

COURSES IN THE PRELIMINARY CERTIFICATE PROGRAM

OLD TESTAMENT SURVEY—LAW AND HISTORY

OLD TESTAMENT SURVEY—POETRY AND PROPHECY

NEW TESTAMENT SURVEY

UNDERSTANDING PEOPLE

UNDERSTANDING TEACHING

TEACHING TECHNIQUES

SUNDAY SCHOOL SUCCESS

SEVENTH EDITION

Third Printing 1978

ISBN O-910566-05-4

CONTENTS

INTRODUCTION

Good Christian education results in the church effectively communicating the Word of God. Capable leaders who minister through teaching are needed if the church is to experience spiritual growth and to advance the program of God.

Leadership begins with dedication and vital concern. It is aided by preparation and understanding. Church leadership preparation includes training in communication. *Teaching Techniques* was written to help provide this training.

A good teacher has been defined as "a person filled with his subject overflowing to others." However, a good teacher does more than this. An informed person also must direct the flow of abounding truth so that benefits can be appropriated by those he teaches. This book helps the teacher channel the truths he presents so the purposes of God are fulfilled and the needs of students met.

Teaching Techniques is used by thousands of churches in the preparation of leaders and teachers. This revised edition incorporates current educational emphases. Each chapter concludes with content review questions, discussion topics, and practical projects.

Teaching Techniques is profitable reading for anyone interested in teaching the Word. When used as a textbook in class instruction, a teacher's guide, overhead transparencies, and a cassette are available to assist the instructor.

This edition retains the impact of Dr. Benson's original presentation. The revision is the work of the Rev. D. K. Reisinger, Dr. George Konrad, and the Association editorial staff.

The book is an integral part of the Evangelical Teacher Training Association program of teacher preparation. When courses are taught by instructors approved by E.T.T.A., the student receives credit applicable to the Association's Teachers Certificate. A further explanation of this program of leadership education is found on page 96 under the caption "Concerning E.T.T.A."

Paul E. Loth, Ed.D., *President*
Evangelical Teacher Training Association

CHAPTER ONE

THE TEACHER HIMSELF

The teacher himself is the key to successful teaching.

Successful Christian teaching begins with the teacher. It involves personal talent, preparation, and a right relationship with God.

Tools and techniques are important. A good teacher knows and uses them. But he is the key to their effectiveness in communicating spiritual truth.

The work of the teacher is filled with rich opportunities to help others and to influence lives. For the Christian teacher, eternal values are involved and the teacher's life style becomes interwoven with the teaching process.

Since teaching is so related to the teacher himself, this opening chapter presents suggestions for personal enrichment for those who desire to be successful teachers.

THE TEACHER'S COMMISSION

The teacher's commission and goals are found in the words of Christ, "Go ye therefore, and teach (make disciples of) all nations . . . teaching them to observe all things whatsoever I have commanded you . . ."[1] The commission to teach is direct and simple — go and teach. It involves the making of disciples and it centers in the teachings of Christ.

The educational goal is that those taught might "observe all things," or put into practice what is taught. It goes beyond simple listening, and asks for more than memorizing certain truths. The teacher is teaching for results in the lives of his pupils. Christ did far more than impart knowledge. His teaching changed the activities of those He taught. Here, then, is the teacher's charter from his Lord. The ministry of teaching is a holy calling.

Christ was a successful teacher. He had something to teach. He wanted to teach. He taught with enthusiasm and authority. He possessed the desires and goals of a teacher. And He has inspired Christians of every generation to teach others also.

THE TEACHER'S LIFE

Every Christian teacher who wants to be used of God faces three important questions: Is my way of life God-exalting? Is my message Christ-centered? Is my teaching Spirit-empowered? The teacher who can answer yes to each of these will contribute much to the teaching ministry of the church. He, as Paul, will be able to say, "For our gospel came not unto you in word only, but also in power, and in the Holy Ghost, and in much assurance; as ye know what manner of men we were among you for your sake."[2]

Four important factors in successful teaching are directly related to the teacher. They include his Christian experience, the commitment of his personality to Christ, the example of his life style, and his relationship to those he teaches.

Christian Experience

At its simplest level, teaching is sharing with others that which has been experienced. To communicate Christ and His message, the teacher must know Jesus Christ as Savior and Lord.

When asked to suggest some of the world's greatest salesmen, a leading merchant listed Paul, Luther, Wesley, Whitefield, Spurgeon, and Moody. "These men were eminently successful as salesmen," he wrote, "because they had implicit faith in the house they represented, and perfect confidence that its goods were absolutely needed. This inspired them with a courage and enthusiasm that demanded and secured attention, and they were kept busy filling orders."

Today's Christian teacher represents the same Christ. There is the same need for God's Word. Success, likewise, depends upon the enthusiasm the teacher has for the task, and his enthusiasm will be in proportion to his own personal faith.

Faith In God

The faith of a Christian teacher goes beyond simple belief in God. It must be an active, vital faith in the Lord Jesus Christ—a triumphant, aggressive faith. The faith of an effective Christian teacher must be a working faith.

Faith In The Bible

Again and again Jesus said, "It is written." He knew that "holy men of God spake as they were moved by the Holy Ghost."[3] Effective preachers, evangelists, and church teachers derive their convictions through unswerving faith in the written Word of God. They do not have enthusiastic assurance unless they believe the Bible is the Word of God. God has written to man: "All Scripture is given by inspiration of God," and the marvel and the wonder of that message should stir the heart of every teacher.

Faith In God's Call

A teacher must realize that he has been called by God to teach. This God-ordained ministry is extremely important because this is God's method to accomplish His purpose on earth. The knowledge that God has set a person aside for this task provides dynamic motivation and assures success.

Personality

A person who commits himself to God strengthens his own personality. His powers are enriched by the Lord and Creator of life. Paul's life was made useful and effective by his surrender to Jesus. Because of his deep experience of the reality of the gospel, he became more open about the needs of his own life[4] and more concerned about the needs of others. Everyone who came into contact with him was influenced by his life because the power of the Holy Spirit was evident. Every Christian teacher needs to grow toward a mature, Christ-like personality.

Example

A teacher's example either contradicts or underscores what he teaches. The teacher's attitude and the unplanned things he says and does make strong impressions on his pupils. This is sometimes called incidental teaching, but it is exceedingly important.

The teacher may emphasize the importance of God's Word, but if he always teaches from a lesson book, he contradicts what he says. He may teach that the offering is an act of worship, but if he hurries through it, he cancels out his teaching. The teacher may speak about love, but if he is unpleasant to his fellow teachers or his family, he cannot teach with real results. The teacher's example is a vital part of the teaching process.

Relationships

The quality of a teacher's relationships with those he teaches also is a determining factor in his success. Teaching involves the personal relationship and close association of instructor and pupil. Long after facts are forgotten, the love of the teacher is remembered. A teacher cannot pretend concern for the welfare of his pupils, nor will a lack of it go unnoticed. The rich young ruler who rejected Christ's teaching still carried with him the assurance of Christ's love.

THE TEACHER'S KNOWLEDGE

The teacher who recognizes the importance of his position seeks to be qualified to fill his place. Those who appreciate the teacher's office also understand the need for preparation.

Professional men spend years in hard study and application. A doctor will not have time to "look it up" when a patient's artery is severed and his life blood is flowing away. The doctor must know what to do or a life will be lost. A mistake would be tragic. So, also, is the blunder of a teacher who gives the wrong counsel regarding spiritual truths.

Teaching periods are all too brief. Every minute must be turned to the best possible use. Only the trained teacher can utilize these precious moments to the best advantage. For this reason, every teacher needs adequate preparation in each of the following areas.

The Bible

To teach the Bible effectively, a teacher needs a working knowledge of the sixty-six books. He should be familiar with all, especially as they relate to Christ. In his teaching, Paul frequently referred to Christ as the example to be followed. He was not satisfied to state principles. He gave down-to-earth examples from the life of Christ to encourage Christian living.

In order to teach love Paul said, "Walk in love, as Christ also hath loved us, and hath given himself. . . "[5] He illustrated unselfishness. "Let every one of us please his neighbor for his good to edification. For even Christ pleased not himself; but, as it is written, The reproaches of them that reproached thee fell on me."[6] He clarified the meaning of humility. "Let this mind be in you, which was also in Christ Jesus. . ."[7]

Paul's teaching was successful because the Holy Spirit was his power. I Thessalonians 1:5 says that Paul spoke in power and in the Holy Spirit. This empowerment was to present the Word.

Today's teacher must teach the message of the Word of God faithfully and, as Paul, in the power of the Spirit. He is not called to teach *a* message from the Bible, but *the* message of the Bible. Only in this way will he change the lives of others.[8]

Related Subjects

In addition to a knowledge of the Bible, the teacher should be familiar with related subjects such as geography, history, and ancient culture.

Geography

Students need to know the geography of Bible lands. New interest is added when they can identify and visualize the mountains, rivers, and towns. But before students can be taught these facts, the teacher must know them.

History

Students are greatly helped when their teacher is well informed about world historical events that parallel the narratives of the Bible. The skillful teacher is able to open up whole new realms of information and interest. He shows them how Bible history and geography fit into secular subjects. He helps them see that "it is history alone, which, without involving us in actual danger, will mature our judgment and prepare us to take right views."[9]

Teachers should become familiar with the historical background of the places in Palestine that have been immortalized by the footsteps of the Lord Jesus Christ.

ANCIENT CULTURE

Life and customs of the ancients differ widely from those of our day. A working knowledge of habits, customs, ceremonies, and attitudes of Bible times helps the teacher enrich lessons and make them live.

Pupil Characteristics

The teacher should know people in general and especially his own pupils. Only then will he find an entrance into their lives. "The child mind," states one educator, "is a citadel that can be taken neither by stealth nor by storm; but there is a natural way of approach and a gate of easy entry always open to him who knows how to find it."

In seeking to understand his pupils, the teacher must be sensitive to the needs of the class. He must be prepared to deal with discipline problems resulting from his own leadership and others caused by faulty home conditions. The teacher needs skill in dealing with people and understanding of broad social problems faced by class members.

The teacher, therefore, takes advantage of every opportunity to understand the needs and backgrounds of those he teaches. A course such as *Understanding People*[10] can provide a good basic knowledge of the characteristics of the various age groups. Then the teacher builds on this broad understanding by his efforts to know individual pupils through meaningful records, planned class contacts, and home visitation.

An extensive study provides evidence that teachers are more effective and have better relationships with pupils if they have knowledge of them in five areas: health, abilities, ambitions, special problems, and cultural milieu.[11]

Techniques of Teaching

Textbooks and manuals are valuable aids, but they never can take the place of a trained teacher. Audiovisuals are effective in imparting information, but they, too, are subordinate to the qualified teacher. Any minister rejoices in the help of consecrated Bible teachers. But dedication and knowledge of the Bible, essential as they are for good teaching, need the third ingredient which is *how* to teach if teachers are going to gain and hold student interest.

Organizations for Church Education

Christian education has expanded. Today's teacher must recognize that there is a growing number of important agencies for education in the church. Together these agencies perform the nurturing function of the church. Teachers and officers must understand the mission of the church and be able to fit their agency and program into the broader and total concern.

Contemporary Conditions

Teaching takes place in the context of the world in which we live—social, political, economic, religious, personal. All these relationships must be understood by the Christian teacher. The Bible message must be related to the present world of the learner. The urgent concerns of the present cannot be avoided or overlooked.

THE TEACHER'S RESPONSIBILITY

The responsibilities of a teacher can be a delight or a drudgery. Systematic preparation procedures will enrich the entire teaching experience. The observance of the three following steps will increase effectiveness of preparation and teaching.

A Right Attitude

The teacher's attitude toward his responsibility will largely determine his success. He has accepted a teaching assignment, not only because of need, but because he is called of God. In exercising his gift of teaching he sees the potential for change in the lives of other persons. God will be working through him to accomplish the mission of the church.

Self Preparation

If a teacher is physically fit, mentally alert, spiritually alive, and socially adept he will find his class a satisfying pleasure.

Physically Fit

Teaching can be greatly enhanced through vibrant, healthy bodies that exhibit zest and zeal. Christ came "that they might have life, and that they might have it more abundantly."[12] Physical fitness requires a surrender of our bodies to Christ[13] as well as constant discipline.

Mentally Alert

An alert mind is essential to successful teaching. Today's students learn to reason logically. They are frustrated by superficial reasoning in church education. The teacher must think intelligently and analyze carefully. He dare not be behind the times. He must read Christian magazines, current events, newspapers, devotional literature, Christian fiction.

SPIRITUALLY ALIVE

It is not enough to study the Bible without personal application. The teacher's fidelity to a daily time of communion with God will enable him to present instruction forcibly. To have the power to be quiet and masterful under every circumstance the teacher must "pray without ceasing." Constant fellowship with God will guarantee the poise which is essential in influencing the lives of others.

SOCIALLY ADEPT

An important area of growth for the teacher is his ability to relate meaningfully to other persons. His class members see in him a deep sense of genuineness, honesty, and acceptance. He is not a manipulator of other people's lives, but one who openly shares himself and that which God has given him.

Lesson Preparation

DEFINITE TIMES FOR STUDY

Certain hours should be set aside each week for lesson preparation. Teaching is so important that its preparation must not be regulated to the spare moments that are left after everything else has received attention.

SPECIFIC PROGRAM OF STUDY

Time will be saved and far more accomplished if the teacher establishes a definite, clearly outlined pattern for study. Bible study opens many avenues of interest. The teacher may be tempted to follow inviting bypaths that are not directly associated with the lesson. However, an orderly plan of procedure will make it possible to accomplish much more in a given period of time.

SUMMARY

The basic question regarding effective teaching relates to the teacher himself. The answer to "Who am I?" precedes the response to "What skills do I possess?" The teaching function of the church has its origin in God. He calls persons to teach and provides the enabling spiritual gifts. It is the teacher's responsibility to exercise and develop these gifts if he is to be a successful teacher.

NOTES

1. Matthew 28:19, 20
2. I Thessalonians 1:5
3. II Peter 1:21
4. I Timothy 1:15
5. Ephesians 5:2
6. Romans 15:2, 3
7. Philippians 2:5
8. II Timothy 4:2
9. Arthur Bestor, *The Restoration of Learning* (New York: Alfred A. Knopf, 1955), p. 133.
10. J. Omar Brubaker and Robert E. Clark, *Understanding People* (Wheaton, Ill.: Evangelical Teacher Training Association, 1972).
11. Robert N. Bush, *The Teacher-Pupil Relationship* (New York: Prentice Hall, 1954), pp. 97, 189.
12. John 10:10
13. Romans 12:1, 2

THINK

1. What important teaching principles can be observed from Christ's commission?
2. What can we learn from Paul regarding basic teaching principles?
3. How does a teacher instruct by his life?
4. Discuss three objects of personal faith which lead to successful teaching.
5. Why is training necessary for every teacher and leader?
6. Name the major areas in which the teacher should have understanding.
7. State three Bible-related subjects with which the teacher should be familiar.
8. What three steps will increase a teacher's effectiveness of preparation and teaching?

TALK

1. Discuss the problems resultant from a church using teachers who do not have a dedicated relationship to Christ. In what ways can the interest of unqualified volunteers be retained?
2. Discuss the qualities of teachers who have impressed group members. Illustrate the qualities which can be emulated. What qualities should be avoided?

ACT

1. Prepare a list of ways your Bible knowledge can be increased during the coming year. Specify when you will relate to each way.
2. Take inventory of your own qualifications to teach. Write two of your best qualifications and two of your greatest needs with respect to teaching. Specify in what ways these needs can be met.

CHAPTER TWO

AIMS IN TEACHING

A teaching aim leads to teaching achievement.

Why teach? Why all the lesson preparation and class sessions? Because the Bible states that believers should be "teaching every man in all wisdom; that we may present every man perfect in Christ Jesus."[1] If this broad goal is to be achieved. aims for each lesson must be determined early in lesson preparation and clearly stated.

VALUE OF AIMS

The importance of aims in the teaching-learning process is seen in the functions they perform. An aim is a clear statement of what the teacher hopes to accomplish by teaching the lesson.

The aim has several purposes. It gives direction to the lesson and helps determine the teaching method to be employed. It leads to the wise utilization of class time and is a basis for evaluation of teaching. It helps in planning, teaching, and evaluating.

In Planning

The aim is directional. Every aspect of the teaching hour should lead toward fulfillment of the established aim. The teaching plan proceeds step by step through introduction, content material, conclusion, and application with each part relating to the aim. Without a stated aim the entire lesson may be as haphazard as the first raindrops in a summer storm.

The aim also helps determine the teaching method which will be used. On the basis of a clearly stated aim, the teacher effectively selects methods and materials. The activities of the class vary with different aims. Whether to lecture, or tell a story, or introduce a discussion is determined on the basis of aims. A project may help students acquire certain skills; a word-by-word study of the text may help them increase their understanding of a doctrine; a general discussion about a critical question may provide greater tolerance of different points of view. Innovative methods often help accomplish aims.

In Teaching

A clearly defined aim also allows the teacher greater flexibility in the class presentation. Changing conditions in the classroom, the unexpected questions, the sudden interest in a special topic, even the time to close can best be handled by the teacher who has an aim clearly in mind. Each element which appears becomes an additional opportunity to direct pupils toward the achievement of the lesson aim.

In Evaluating

One of the great needs for the Christian teacher is to be able to evaluate the results of his teaching. Evaluation is a necessary part of all teaching activities. In order to be able to measure results, a clear teaching aim is required. Few pleasures compare with the joy of the teacher who sees helpful changes taking place in the lives of his class members. As he recognizes these to be a fulfillment of his teaching aims, he is encouraged to serve the Lord with greater zeal and enthusiasm.

BASES FOR AIMS

There are essentially two bases for determining a teaching aim. One is the content of the biblical portion of the lesson which is being taught. The other is the need of the learner.

The Word of God

To determine biblical aims it is necessary for the teacher to become a serious student of the Bible. He will read and reread the passage until it becomes a part of his life. He will seek to understand the context and the situation in which it was written so that he can clearly state the objective truth it offers.

Class Members

Another basis for the teaching aim is the need of the learner. A teacher must be careful to establish aims which are true to the text and also apply to the learner's situation.

Establishing teaching aims directed to the situation of the pupils is a great responsibility. In the final analysis the teacher will determine what will happen in the classroom. Unless he is willing to take the time and expend the effort to know his class members, his effectiveness will be seriously limited. He must spend much time in prayer to seek God's will concerning which truth of the Bible he will emphasize and which needs of the learners he will seek to meet.

GENERAL AIMS OF CHURCH TEACHING

The teacher's major responsibility is that of transmitting the Word of God so that every pupil may be transformed by God's grace.

Lead Pupils to Christ

The Christian teacher must recognize and know his responsibility to lead each pupil to trust in Christ and accept Him as personal Savior. The teacher should explain the way of salvation as revealed in God's Word. He should pray for each pupil and seek to bring him to a clear, biblical faith in Christ. Such decisions may come spontaneously as the culmination of careful teaching. The teacher should never use artificial, high-pressure methods, especially in dealing with young children.

Acceptance of Christ as Savior is the first step toward a full life. The Christian teacher also will seek to lead those who receive Christ to continuous growth in Christian living.

Present the Eternal Purpose of God

The abundant Christian life is the theme of the Christian teacher. "Eye hath not seen, nor ear heard, neither have entered into the heart of man, the things which God hath prepared for them that love him. But God hath revealed them unto us by His Spirit; for the Spirit searcheth all things, yea, the deep things of God."[2] It is the Christian teacher's privilege to show God's gracious and glorious purpose for His children and explain the far-reaching happiness that is the portion of every child of God.

Guide Each Pupil to Fulfill God's Will

God has a plan for every Christian. His Word gives directions for knowing His will. The teacher must obey the divine commission: "Feed my lambs."[3] Young Christians must "grow in grace, and in the knowledge of our Lord and Saviour Jesus Christ."[4] Christian character results from knowing God's Word, obeying His will, and continually acknowledging Jesus Christ as Lord. This requires daily fellowship with God through prayer. The teacher instructs his students in these realities of Christian growth.

WORSHIP

Worship is the Christian's experience of ascribing worth to God. In worship believers adore God and contemplate His holy perfection. Worship is fellowship with God. It is part of the teacher's work to cultivate the worship experience of his pupils through class sessions and the services of the church. Instruction should be given in the meaning of reverence, gratitude, love, and faith. This should include songs, stories, and prayers best suited to the age and experience of the group.

Such training requires that pupils be given opportunity to worship as a means of expression. The Word of God bears a vital relationship to such instruction. The entire Bible abounds in expressions which provide acceptable forms of devotion.

Consistent Christian Living

Pupils' lives reveal a measure of teacher success or failure. New life in Christ should result in efforts to honor Christ in daily living. An essential guide toward this is patient, dedicated teaching of the Word of God. It is, therefore, the teacher's responsibility to link the truths taught with the daily lives of the pupils to help them to be "doers of the word, and not hearers only."[5] Christians who possess the truth as well as profess it will be transformed.

The impartation of knowledge does not complete the Christian educational process . . . For education to be effective, it must lead to action . . . Christian education in the deepest sense takes place in a God-conscious atmosphere. If the Holy Spirit is present to inform, to convict, and to inspire —if He has breathed on the teacher and the pupils, there will be a sense of alertness, aliveness, and anticipation that otherwise will be lacking.[6]

Christian character is formed as people respond in obedience to the Word of God. The teacher has the responsibility of imparting the Word. As God speaks, pupils will respond, and the Holy Spirit will effect growth in grace and in the knowledge of Jesus Christ.

Christian Service

Service to the Lord is one manifestation of spiritual growth. The alert teacher plans and initiates such activities in the home, the church, and the community.

Jesus was particularly concerned about the needs of people. He healed the sick, comforted the sorrowing, and helped the oppressed. The growing Christian increases in his concern for others.

The church provides many service opportunities. Teachers, officers, board members, ushers, singers are needed. All these activities can become mature expressions of Christian service.

SPECIFIC AIMS OF CHURCH TEACHING

Aims for the same lesson can vary according to the emphasis which is needed. At times the purpose will be to increase factual knowledge. At other times it will be to improve attitudes. Often it will be to lead to action and change behavior.

Each of these three kinds of aims is necessary in the teaching process. The teacher will choose the one (s) most appropriate to the biblical text and the needs of his pupils.

To Increase Knowledge

Accumulation of information or gathering of facts is a basic level of learning in church education. Christianity includes a body of knowledge which is essential for the learner to know and understand before he can make a commitment to Christ. The historic facts of Christ's life, death, and resurrection are at the heart of the gospel. The story of God's acts in the history of the Jews as recorded in the Old Testament provides a necessary framework for the Christian faith. The teachings of the apostles convey doctrinal truth of significance for the believer.

However, by themselves knowledge and understanding are not enough. Certainly the scribes and Pharisees were the best informed "believers" of their time. Yet Christ said, "Except your righteousness shall exceed the righteousness of the scribes and Pharisees, ye shall in no case enter into the kingdom of heaven."[7] Knowledge is not the equivalent of the Christian life; understanding is not an assurance of Christian maturity. To be sure pupils learn biblical facts a specific knowledge aim might be established for each lesson. This will state what facts of Scripture students should know at the completion of the lesson.

To Improve Attitudes

Learners not only have the capacity for knowledge, they also have the ability to feel. The teaching aim to change attitudes deals essentially with emotions and desires. It is not enough for an individual to know that a certain type of behavior is sinful. Until he feels deeply that it is wrong, he will continue in that type of behavior. Attitudes are the springboard for changes in behavior.

Attitudes deal with ideals and with convictions. An individual may be willing to die for a cause but not simply for certain information he possesses. Attitudes are closely connected with interpersonal relationships and exposure to the attitudes of others. Every Christian teacher desires the development of attitudes which reflect the values of Jesus Christ. Attitudes are more likely improved if a teacher distinctly aims his lesson toward a specific attitude change.

To Change Behavior

The Christian teacher also is concerned about a change of behavior. He is not satisfied with the increase of knowledge; he cannot rest with an improvement of attitudes; he must strive for change of behavior in the lives of his pupils.

The Bible emphasizes action. Jesus said, "Blessed are they

that hear the word of God, and keep it."[8] Even faith is considered dead when appropriate action is not forthcoming. Since behavior change can be recognized, an action aim for a lesson can be clearly stated.

DEFINING SPECIFIC AIMS

An effective aim has the following characteristics:
Brief enough to be remembered
Specific enough to meet needs
Clear enough to be obvious
Practical enough to be attainable
Interesting enough to provoke participation
Pertinent enough to undergird the unit.[9]

Aims are more easily accomplished if they are clearly enough defined to be written prior to the lesson presentation. They should be achievable and the degree to which the aim is achieved should be measurable. Sometimes specific aims can be stated in actual measurable terms.

A knowledge aim would read, "That the pupils learn the books of the Old Testament as shown by their ability to locate the books in a Bible drill."

An aim for attitude improvement might read, "That the attitude of children will improve regarding the significance of a worship period as shown by some boys being willing to help receive the offering."

In preparing an action aim in relation to the doctrine of the church, a teacher might state, "That pupils will cooperate with the church as shown by at least three-fourths of the class attending church service today."

If specific aims are met in individual lessons, the possibility of general aims for the unit or year being met is increased.

SUMMARY

Clearly defined aims are essential for effective teaching. General aims of every teacher are to lead pupils to confess Christ as Lord and Savior and to grow in Christian maturity toward Christlikeness. These general aims become effective in the teaching-learning process as they are translated into specific lesson aims on the basis of the Scripture passage and the needs of the pupils. The specific types of aims for teaching effectiveness are to increase knowledge, to improve attitudes, and to change behavior.

NOTES

1. Colossians 1:28
2. I Corinthians 2:9, 10
3. John 21:15
4. II Peter 3:18
5. James 1:22
6. T. B. Maston, *Christianity and World Issues* (San Antonio, Tex.: Naylor Co., 1951), p. 343.
7. Matthew 5:20
8. Luke 11:28
9. John T. Sisemore, *Blueprint for Teaching* (Nashville: Broadman Press, 1964), p. 56.

THINK

1. What is the major responsibility of a church teacher?
2. What is an aim?
3. What is the multiple purpose of the aim?
4. In what three functions is the value of aims shown?
5. On what two bases are aims determined?
6. Identify the three kinds of aims.
7. Why is the aim of changing behavior so important?
8. What are the three general aims of church teaching?

TALK

1. Basing discussion on Luke 7:36-50, consider an appropriate knowledge aim, attitude aim, and behavior aim for the passage. Discuss how the selection of any one of the aims will change the lesson emphasis.
2. Discuss how fully lesson aims should be known to pupils. Will revealing aims motivate or build barriers?

ACT

1. Visit a class in session. Inquire in advance what the aims of the lesson are. Throughout the session observe the teacher's methods and procedures to fulfill these aims.
2. Select a lesson in a quarterly and mark each place the lesson emphasis clearly leads to fulfillment of the stated aim. Indicate any aims you feel should be changed.

CHAPTER THREE

METHODS OF TEACHING

Teaching methods are imperative knowledge for church teachers.

Mastering biblical materials brings joy and satisfaction to the teacher. However, he must be able to share insights and enthusiasm with his class members. To do this he must select an appropriate teaching method from an almost endless variety available. Often he will use several methods in one teaching period. The selection depends on the abilities of the teacher, the characteristics and needs of the pupils, the teaching material, available equipment and facilities.

In this chapter some major teaching methods are outlined. Successful teaching requires proficiency in the use of several of them.

STORYTELLING

Telling a story is a favorite method of teaching children; however, it can be used effectively with any age group. Jesus was a master storyteller. His stories are unsurpassed as models of character painting by means of action and spoken word.

A good story is interesting, dramatic, full of action, and true to life. Because narrative arouses interest at the outset, probably there is no better method to gain and hold attention. The Bible as a whole is a thrilling, fascinating message much of which can be presented in story form.

Most Bible stories possess conflict, plot, suspense—the characteristics that make a dramatic story. In retelling these stories, verbs will abound, but adjectives should be used sparingly. Sentences must be short and language simple. By look, gesture, and facial expression the teacher portrays truth, gaining immediate attention through the eyegate.

A good story is action packed. It is full of action, but not full of words. Often action is intensified by the restriction of words. The stories Jesus told emphasize achievement. He does not take time to describe His characters, but each character is clearly pictured by his deeds. The story of the Good Samaritan in Luke 10 illustrates this principle.

The impossible seldom appeals. But achievement which is possible for a child interests him. While a fairy tale develops the pupil's imagination, the true story commands larger interest because it is within the realm of realization. It is the element of truth that characterizes Bible stories and makes them superior to all others.

Storytelling provides the pupil with an opportunity to share in the experiences of people of the past. He can feel the pain of Adam and Eve as they are driven out of Eden. He can sense the despair of David as he cries for his son, Absalom. He can share in the joy of the father as he embraces his prodigal son.

Several important factors must be kept in mind if one is to become an effective storyteller:

> Careful choice, study of the story itself and perhaps of its background, outlining its characters and the sequence of events mentally or in writing, memorizing key or beautifully written phrases or paragraphs, practicing the telling (at least once *aloud*), telling it in relaxed fashion and with enjoyment.[1]

Stories do not just happen. They develop with hard work and diligent practice. In every story a certain structure must be observed. There is an introduction, growing action, the climax, and a quick ending.

The Beginning

The beginning of the story must gain interest, introduce the main characters, and get the action started. Luke 15:11 and 12 provide the beginning for the story of the prodigal son.

The Growing Action

A series of rhetorical questions and answers, problems and solutions are used to carry the story on and capture the attention of the listener. In the prodigal son we see the main actor leave home, spend his money, go bankrupt, and come to himself in quick sequence. The action increases until the listeners feel that they must know the outcome.

The Climax

What is the final answer? Will the son really apologize? Will his father throw him out? He certainly deserves it! But to our amazement "his father . . . ran, and fell on his neck, and kissed him."[2]

The Ending

The ending is short and to the point. It provides a picture of the final outcome and then stops.

RECITATION OR IMMEDIATE CLASS PARTICIPATION

Intellectual development requires more than listening. Pupils fed only with stories will not grow mentally.

Listening must give way to more active participation. The pupil must become involved if there is to be assimilation and reproduction. Education is in reality a drawing-out process, and for this reason class participation through recitation can be of real advantage.

Preparation for recitation encourages the pupil to develop his own initiative. It enables him to come to class with some familiarity of the subject. It provides an opportunity for the teacher to learn the pupil's acquaintance with the truth and to discover erroneous thinking on his part. The pupil frequently is helped to clarify his own thinking by orally expressing himself in class. In the event a class member appears intellectually lazy, the teacher has opportunity to challenge him to active participation.

No recitation is successful if conducted simply as routine. To insist that the pupil merely recite in the language of the textbook dulls his originality and fails to call forth any activity except that of memory.

There are three major parts to the recitation method: the assignment, the pupil's study, and the class participation.

The Assignment

If assignments are to lead to successful recitation sessions, they must be clearly understood by the student and assigned sufficiently in advance to allow time for good preparation. The assignment should lead to information of evident worth.

Pupil Preparation

Much depends upon motivation by the teacher as to whether home assignments are boring or adventuresome. Arousing interest and causing the pupil to see the benefits of accomplishment are key factors. Assignments within the range of individual abilities and available time are more frequently completed. The cooperative interest of parents should be cultivated, so that pupils will be encouraged to complete home study.

Class Participation

Time should be allowed for class contributions on the basis of assignments. If time is divided judiciously there can be wide participation. Each contribution should be related to the overall lesson emphasis. Carefully tying together the work of various pupils enriches each part. Sharing discoveries of those well-prepared pupils benefits all.

DISCUSSION

The discussion method produces pupil involvement by requiring interpretation of the lesson. This prevents pupils from acquiring knowledge without appropriating it. It aids in a continuous development or gradual construction of the lesson and stimulates the spirit of inquiry and personal interest. No other method is as well adapted for securing individual expression or application of the lesson.

The discussion method is more than an interpupil or pupil-teacher debate. It also goes beyond asking pointed questions and receiving answers. Discussion is an attempt on the part of the entire group to reach understanding in some area, to find the solution to a problem, to clarify an idea, or to determine a course of action.

Pupils will soon perceive whether the teacher is introducing a genuine discussion or merely providing an opportunity for some class opinion before he gives the final and definitive answer. For a discussion to be productive an atmosphere of friendliness and openness must prevail. Profitable discussion is based on a respect for the opinion of each person present. It is an honest invitation by the leader to others to participate in a common cause.

The teacher's role is more difficult in leading a discussion than in almost any other teaching method. It requires careful preparation and skillful guidance. There must be a background of experience and a fund of knowledge to creatively lead a discussion.

Although the question or problem to be discussed may be raised by a pupil, or introduced by the teacher, the discussion will be more interesting if it presents an actual problem related to the felt needs of the class. It is important that the problem be stated in such a way that all will understand its nature and significance.

During the discussion the leader will use questions and comments to focus on the central issue and move the discussion forward. Occasionally, he will need to review and summarize what has been said, or the conclusions suggested thus far. Throughout the discussion he will set the tone. He will be sensitive to the need to limit those who may be too talkative or to encourage those who hesitate to contribute.

The teacher will also provide general resources in materials and needed information. In a theological or biblical discussion, he should be ready to suggest related passages and other sources of information. This does not mean that he will be the "answer man." Rather, he will help the participants find answers.

Many discussions lead to decisions concerning action. One writer has suggested the following steps in such a discussion.

A careful understanding of the problem.
Possible ways of meeting the problem.
A decision on definite action.
Setting up the instruments for carrying out the decisions: appointing committee, deciding on dates, etc.
Carrying through the decision.
An evaluation of results.[3]

The discussion method will be most successfully used with youth and adults. However, it is also a delightful experience to enter into a discussion with children. Often they surprise their leaders with profound questions and theological insights.

PROJECT

The project method can be used successfully in Christian education. A project is essentially a purposeful activity which the student plans because he is interested in it. He gathers information about it and carries the project to completion.

The project should have teaching value as well as practical application. Usually the project is started in the class period, but completed during the week at home.

The project method gives the pupil opportunity to learn by doing. Cooperation, tolerance of others' opinions, initiative, responsibility, alertness, and judgment are developed. This method strengthens character and provides opportunity to acquire and develop skills.

The research project helps the student become an independent investigator. Here the teacher assigns each class member a part of the lesson to investigate for himself. During the lesson period class members present their reports. These are commented upon, evaluated, and organized under the direction of the teacher. This method is especially effective for adolescent and adult classes. Successful reporting strengthens the value of the research.

Reports should be brief, correlated, and followed by a summary of the findings. If the reports clearly relate to each other interest will be aroused and sustained. The teacher can accomplish this by making suitable assignments and distributing them to the best advantage.

LECTURE

The lecture method has long been used by many teachers. It permits the teaching of a large class and allows close adherence to the teacher's planned presentation. It often is an uninterrupted, connected discourse, leading to a predetermined conclusion. Both time and effort are saved, since no time is wasted getting to the point or waiting for class response. There is no danger of being side-tracked by an unexpected suggestion from the class. The lecture method permits smooth, easy, direct, and systematic development of the lesson. However, if the class does not follow the lecturer, and think with him, all these advantages are lost. Mental growth, as spiritual and physical, comes through activity and this can be assured only when the pupil contributes to the development of the lesson.

The lecture method requires thorough preparation, since the effectiveness of the lecture depends upon the careful use of material, illustrations, and supporting evidence. In the actual lecture the teacher must avoid rambling. He must vary his manner, speak clearly, use the language of the listeners, lead the pupils to the realization and solution of problems. He also must insert good illustrations and examples, use humor occasionally, and watch for audience reaction.

The effectiveness of lectures can be increased by planning for overt class participation. If the class size and teaching situation permit, a teacher can intersperse his lecture with pupil reactions, comments, questions, and discussions.

Pupils may be given advance reading and research assignments relating to the lecture topic. Or, they may be provided with a series of questions and listen for the answers in the lecture. Another approach is to have the students write the lecture outline and then compare it with that of the teacher. A lecture can be successfully culminated by an evaluation session in which students and teacher evaluate the contents and the learning that has taken place.

INDUCTIVE BIBLE STUDY

Inductive Bible study, which is very profitable in individual study, may also be used as a group method of teaching and learning. The inductive method leads participants to discover Bible truths themselves. When inductive Bible study is used with a group, the leader serves primarily as a coordinator and resource person.

Basically, there are three steps in the inductive method: observation (what does it say?), interpretation (what does it mean?), and application (what does it mean to me?).[4]

Observation

The first step in inductive Bible study for either individual or group is to discover exactly what the author has written. A simple method is for each to write the Scripture passage in one column, verse by verse, and phrase by phrase. In a second column observations can be recorded. Another column can be used by the pupil to write questions he might have. Observations and questions then become the basis for group discussion. If these columns are completed prior to class time, the discussion becomes the means of initiating the lesson.

The following chart illustrates these divisions.

Scripture Passage	Observation	Questions
I Corinthians 13:1		
Though I speak	author speaking personally	
with the tongues of men and of angels,	tongues of men and of angels	What is the tongue of an angel?
and have not charity,	a missing ingredient	
I am become as sounding brass, or a tinkling cymbal	compared to two instruments	Why these two instruments?

Interpretation

A second step in inductive Bible study is interpretation. The purpose of interpretation is to discover the meaning the author wishes to convey. Seven steps of interpretation have been suggested: pray and meditate, discern, define, compare, investigate, consult, summarize.[5]

Only with the guidance of the Holy Spirit can Scripture be interpreted properly; therefore, prayer and meditation are important and should precede decision.

Meaning can be discerned by asking related questions and seeking answers to these. Questions should be asked of one another as well as by the teacher or leader. Definitions of key words can be found in a dictionary, discussed by the group, and then related to the passage being studied.

A fruitful comparison will be provided by the reading of the passage in different translations and noting differences and similarities. If students are asked in advance to bring various translations to class, they will be prepared to share in this way.

Scriptures often provide their own interpretations. One portion can be compared with another which deals with a similar truth. Bible cross reference or a topical encyclopedia provide helps for this. Commentaries should be used only after some preliminary decision concerning the meaning of the passage is reached.

In a few statements the main meaning of the Bible passage then can be summarized by each person individually or cooperatively in small groups.

Application

The third step in inductive Bible study sometimes is the most difficult since it faces the participant with God's message. No longer is he merely seeking to understand. Now, he must decide to obey or disobey. This requires prayer and faith but leads to the changing of lives. A teacher can encourage right decision by permitting time for sharing decisions among class members.

SUMMARY

Methodology is one of the most important ingredients in the teaching process. Every teacher should develop as many methods as he can handle successfully.

Storytelling is a time-honored teaching method used extensively by our Lord Jesus. Good stories follow a certain logical and chronological structure. They also are dramatic and true to life.

Another popular method is recitation in which pupils are given extensive opportunities for self-expression. A good method of involving many is the class discussion in which the group faces important questions or problems. The project method helps the student to learn by doing. While the lecture method involves primarily the teacher, it can be combined with other methods to provide class involvement.

Inductive Bible study is a popular current method of studying and teaching the Word. Essentially, this involves an attempt to know what the text says, understand its meaning, and then apply it to the life of the learner.

NOTES

1. Dorothy Fritz, *Ways of Thinking* (Philadelphia: The Westminster Press, 1965), p. 48.
2. Luke 15:20
3. Irene Caldwell, *Teaching That Makes a Difference* (Anderson, Ind.: The Warner Press, rev. 1962), p. 66.
4. Harry G. Coiner, *Teaching the Word to Adults* (St. Louis: Concordia Publishing House, 1962), pp. 87-89.
5. Oletta Wald, *The Joy of Discovery* (Minneapolis: Bible Banner Press, 1956), pp. 29-30.

THINK

1. On what bases should a teacher select a method of teaching?
2. Discuss the major principles in good storytelling.
3. Enumerate the four-fold structure of a good story.
4. List the advantages of using recitation in teaching.
5. What is the teacher's role in leading a discussion?
6. List the values of the project method.
7. How can students become more involved in the lecture method?
8. Name and describe the three steps in inductive Bible study.

TALK

1. Discuss the necessary qualifications of a group discussion leader. Take turns within the group serving as the designated leader during the discussion.
2. With limited class time what portion of the lesson period can justifiably be spent for project reports?

ACT

1. Observing the principles of storytelling, tell a story either to a class or an informal group. Ask a fellow class member to observe group interest and suggest strengths and weaknesses of the presentation.
2. Prepare a Bible study which can be taught in a class situation and which utilizes the inductive method. Arrange to teach this to a class.

CHAPTER FOUR

HOW TO TEACH

The laws of learning do not change but are expressed differently in differing societies.

An old axiom is: "Teachers are born, not made." Present-day educators, however, believe that many so-called natural abilities in reality may be acquired habits. Although some have more teaching gifts than others, teachers can be assured of success if they follow recognized principles of pedagogy, are enthusiastic about teaching, love their pupils, and are thorough in their preparation.

This philosophy does not minimize the work of the Holy Spirit. Every teacher should live a surrendered life and be guided by the Holy Spirit. However, the Holy Spirit is not dishonored by the application of the laws of teaching any more than He is dishonored when we comply with the laws of gravitation.

Our Lord Jesus Christ consistently observed the laws of teaching and learning. These principles can be observed, evaluated, and cataloged because they are inherent in man's make-up. "All things were created by [Christ], and for him: And he is before all things, and by him all things consist."[1] "In [Christ] are hid all the treasures of wisdom and knowledge."[2]

The Seven Laws of Teaching by John Milton Gregory sets the pattern for the work of a teacher by presenting a clear and simple statement of the important factors governing the art of teaching. Gregory was an outstanding educational leader. He was a school teacher at the age of seventeen. Later he became a Baptist minister. He was soon recognized as an educator of superior ability. After serving as state superintendent and as a college president in Michigan, he labored for thirteen years in laying the foundation of the University of Illinois. He has earned a secure place in the history of American education.[3]

The laws of teaching, as given in this chapter, are based on the theories and principles in Dr. Gregory's book.[4]

THE LAW OF THE TEACHER

A TEACHER MUST BE ONE WHO KNOWS THE LESSON OR TRUTH OR ART TO BE TAUGHT.

Some leadership education courses give more attention to the *methods* of the teacher than to the *message* of the Word of

God. This can be dangerous unless the teacher is thoroughly familiar with *what* is to be taught. Methods and message are both important. For this reason, one-half of the Certificate courses of Evangelical Teacher Training Association are devoted to the direct study of the Bible and related subjects. In general education, a knowledge of the subject is essential. In Christian education, it is important that the teacher know the Word of God. Knowledge is the material with which the teacher works. Imperfect knowledge will be reflected in imperfect teaching. What a man does not know, he cannot teach. "Know thoroughly and familiarly the lesson you wish to teach,—teach from a full mind and a clear understanding."[5]

The teacher should know more than he has time to teach, not just enough to fill the time. This requires earnest study and investigation in order to have a grasp of the complete lesson. The teacher who masters his subject can be at ease as he directs the class in its thought and active participation. He should also know each pupil well enough to bring his own knowledge to bear in the life of the pupil.

THE LAW OF THE PUPIL

A LEARNER IS ONE WHO ATTENDS WITH INTEREST TO THE LESSON.

Long before Spurgeon became a great preacher, he was a successful children's worker. In his instructions to his teachers he said, "Get the children's attention. If they do not hearken, you may talk, but you will speak to no purpose whatever. If they do not listen, you go through your labors as an unmeaning drudgery to yourselves and your pupils too. You can do nothing without securing their attention."

"Gain and keep the attention and interest of the pupils upon the lesson. Do not try to teach without attention."[6]

Attention

Cradle roll, nursery, and kindergarten children have only brief attention spans, perhaps one minute for each year. Usually no more should be expected of them. Primary children will have an increasingly lengthened period of sustained attention. They begin to appreciate their own abilities and to enjoy longer periods of thought or discussion. By the middle of the first grade or during the second grade, well-trained school pupils begin to make the transition from much physical activity to the enjoyment of mental activity. Their attention span becomes noticeably lengthened. At any grade level the wise teacher seeks first to gain attention, then to retain it, and finally to turn attention into interest.

Interest

Attention is dependent on interest. It is comparatively easy to gain and hold the attention of an interested pupil. An imperative command or some clever eye-catching trick may temporarily attract attention, but genuine interest alone will sustain it.

Ability to gain and maintain interest will depend on:

discovering the pupil's plane of thought;
guarding against outside distractions;
providing a lesson suited to the pupil's capacity;
enlisting the pupil's cooperation in the lesson.

Attention and interest are directly related to motivation. Motivated learning is learning that is desired by the pupil. The quickest route to motivated learning is by adapting the lesson to the needs of the pupils. If learners are given things to do that seem worthwhile to them and that meet their needs, attention and interest will be maintained.

THE LAW OF THE LANGUAGE

THE LANGUAGE USED AS A MEDIUM BETWEEN TEACHER AND THE LEARNER MUST BE COMMON TO BOTH.

The teacher with his important equipment of knowledge is on the one hand; the pupil with his requisite of interested attention is on the other. The next step is to set up successful communication between them.

The teacher may have a larger vocabulary than the pupil, but he must limit himself to the language of the latter. If the teacher fails or refuses to adjust to the pupil's language, the instruction will not be comprehended. "Use words understood in the same way by the pupils and yourself—language clear and vivid to both."[7]

The language will differ for every age and department in the church. To observe the law of the language Gregory suggests that the teacher:

Study constantly and carefully the language of the pupils.
Express himself as far as possible in their language.
Use the simplest and fewest words that will express his meaning.
Use short sentences of the simplest construction.
Explain the meaning of new words by illustrations.
Test frequently the pupils' understanding of the words he uses.[8]

THE LAW OF THE LESSON

THE LESSON TO BE MASTERED MUST BE EXPLICABLE IN THE TERMS OF TRUTH ALREADY KNOWN BY THE LEARNER—THE UNKNOWN MUST BE EXPLAINED BY MEANS OF THE KNOWN.

This law deals directly with the lesson or truth to be taught. It is fundamental to all pedagogy. "Begin with what is already well known to the pupil upon the subject and with what he has himself experienced,—and proceed to the new material by single, easy, and natural steps, letting the known explain the unknown."[9]

All teaching must begin at a known point of contact. If the subject is entirely new, then a known point must be sought. This law of association or contact is basic for all mental development. New truths can be understood only in terms of the old.

Our Lord was a master of this law. He constantly built new truths on well-known facts. His hearers were familiar with the Old Testament. His crucifixion was to be similar to the lifting up of the brazen serpent in the wilderness. His burial and resurrection were likened to the experiences through which Jonah had passed. The times of His return would be like the days of Noah and the days of Lot. Future events were portrayed in terms of things that had already happened.

To observe the law of the lesson, the teacher should be aware of several related procedures.

Relate to Former Lessons

What has already been studied may be assumed to lie in the realm of the known. If the teacher has taught these former lessons, he will be on familiar ground with his pupils. Every review is a demonstration of this law, and those who emphasize reviews best observe this principle.

Proceed by Graded Steps

An athlete doesn't set his mark at an unattained height and then try to jump it. He starts at a level which he can clear and then advances inch by inch until a new height is established. So a pupil must fully grasp each truth before the next can be explored and understood. New ideas become part of the pupil's knowledge and serve as a starting place for each fresh advance. If the teacher observes this principle, more rapid progress can be made and higher achievement attained.

Illuminate by Illustration

When the advance is too rapid for the mind to follow, reference to known scenes permits the understanding to catch up. Figures of speech, such as similes, metaphors, and allegories, have sprung out of the need for relating old truths and familiar scenes and experiences to the new lesson.

Guide toward Transfer of Learning

The law of the lesson also applies to the transfer of what the pupil has learned in one situation to another. When a pupil has learned to obey his mother or father, will he also obey the Lord?

If the known situation and the unknown are similar and have enough elements in common, the learner may be able to transfer his insight from one situation to another. The teacher has the responsibility to help his pupils see the common elements and the broader application of Bible principles he presents.

THE LAW OF THE TEACHING PROCESS

TEACHING IS AROUSING AND USING THE PUPIL'S MIND TO GRASP THE DESIRED THOUGHT OR TO MASTER THE DESIRED ART.

"There can be no religious integration of the self until the thinker or learner himself is involved in his thought."[10] The pupil should assimilate every portion of the Bible as he is fed. The teacher's activity is not effective until he arouses interest and produces action in the pupil. "Stimulate the pupil's own mind to action. Keep his thoughts as much as possible ahead of your expression, placing him in the attitude of a discoverer."[11]

"The highly personal business of fitting your child to utilize his capacities to the fullest is the direct opposite of the assembly-line process."[12] If pupils do not think for themselves, there will be little lasting result. The learning processes are quickened when pupils become independent investigators. It is true that knowledge can be obtained without a teacher, and some successful, self-made men have never attended schools of higher learning. This does not, however, eliminate the necessity for schools and teachers. The good teacher simply provides favorable conditions for self-learning. He does not merely impart knowledge. He stimulates his pupils to acquire it. He motivates his pupils and sets an example of earnest, serious scholarship. He leads, but he does not stand in the way of his pupils' progress.

Provide Thought Material

Mental processes are limited to the field of acquired knowledge. The pupil who knows nothing cannot think, for he has nothing to think about. In order to compare, criticize, judge, and reason, the mind must work on the material in its own possession. For that reason, the pupil needs factual information which will serve as the basis of thought. Education is in part a drawing out process, but no teacher can draw out knowledge that has not been previously implanted in the pupil's mind.

Provoke Investigation

It is important to arouse the spirit of investigation. Rich educational processes begin when pupils ask who, what, when, why, where, how. The maturing mind grapples with the problems of the universe. The falling apple caused the inquiring mind of Newton to ask the question of gravitation. The boiling teakettle propounded to Watt the problem of a steam engine. The question is both an index to the pupil's mind and an index to his inner self. His question leads to self-realization and self-seeking. The teacher should stimulate this natural quest for knowledge, as well as a natural desire for expression.

Provide Satisfaction

When a pupil derives pleasure from what he is doing, he is more likely to continue the activity. This is known as reward or reenforcement. The tendency is to repeat those experiences which are satisfying and avoid those which are not.

Satisfaction will be provided where learning is helpful to the pupil in his daily life, where it meets his needs. It is the teacher's opportunity to make the learning experience worthwhile for each pupil.

THE LAW OF THE LEARNING PROCESS

LEARNING IS THINKING INTO ONE'S OWN UNDERSTANDING A NEW IDEA OF TRUTH OR WORKING INTO HABIT A NEW ART OR SKILL.

The effective teacher arouses and guides the self-activities of his pupils. He also evaluates the pupil's response to the teacher's efforts. He helps pupils to evaluate new truths and translate them into the arts and skills of basic daily living.

Learning requires active interest and attention, and a clear and distinct act or process which only the pupil can perform. He must cultivate his own mind by his own power to achieve a true concept of the facts or principles of the lesson. This law of the learning process is vital.

The work of education is more the work of the pupil than of the teacher. True learning is more than repetition. Original discovery is a thrilling, stimulating process. The discoverer borrows facts known to others and adds that which he has learned by experience. The teacher uses this law to guide the pupil to be an independent investigator.

There are three distinct stages of learning, each one carrying the pupil toward the mastery of learning.

Reproduction

"Require the pupil to reproduce in thought the lesson he is learning—thinking it out in its various phases and applications till he can express it in his own language."[13] It is possible to reproduce the exact words of any lesson by committing them to memory. However, the pupil who does not understand what he has memorized does not possess the lesson. He is like a man who purchases a book and places it in his library, but makes no use of it.

Interpretation

There is a decided advance in the learning process when the pupil is taught to give more than the actual words or facts that he has learned. When he expresses his own opinion of these facts, he understands what he has been taught. He has learned to deal with his own thoughts as well as the thoughts of others. Failure to insist on original thinking is a most common fault of untrained teachers. A good teacher seldom asks the question what. This calls for only factual answers. A trained teacher asks why so that the pupil learns to think for himself.

Application

Education is more than the acquisition or understanding of knowledge. No lesson is fully learned until it is applied to life. Knowledge is power—but only when it is conquered, harnessed, put to work. Expressing an opinion may exercise the mind, but applying knowledge affects the will and transforms the life of the learner. If practical, personal application is neglected, pupils will be "ever learning, and never able to come to the knowledge of the truth."[14] This is mere "head knowledge" and does not result in the life-changing, transforming operation of the grace of God.

THE LAW OF REVIEW AND APPLICATION

THE TEST AND PROOF OF TEACHING DONE MUST BE A REVIEWING, RETHINKING, REKNOWING, REPRODUCING, AND APPLYING OF THE MATERIAL THAT HAS BEEN TAUGHT.

Business sessions often open with the reading of the minutes of the previous meeting, and close with the minutes of that day's proceedings. There are reviews of what transpired—at the beginning and end of the meeting. The first review establishes close relationship with former sessions. The second carries the day's proceedings into the next assembly. It is important to make contact with former lessons at the beginning of each lesson. It is equally essential that each day's instruction be carried over to the next lesson, and that all learning be vitalized in the lives of the pupils. "Review, *review*, REVIEW, reproducing the old, deepening its impression with new thought, linking it with added meanings, finding new applications, correcting any false views, and completing the true."[15]

This law involves a knowledge and practice of three areas of emphasis.

Strengthen and Perfect Knowledge

Review is more than repetition. It is an attempt to refocus facts and principles which have been learned earlier. It also provides the opportunity to gain deeper insight and tie previous knowledge to new situations. The first viewing of a picture will not reveal every detail. The second reading of a book usually brings out facts that were missed in the preliminary perusal. So it is with Bible study. No other book needs more careful reading and study. No other book is so filled with treasures and blessings. A review of familiar, favorite passages will reveal new light and disclose new lessons.

Remember and Confirm Knowledge

Review familiarizes and strengthens through association of ideas. A person who is introduced to a group of people may not be sure of many of the names. Later, when another stranger is presented, he will review names and his memory will be strengthened. The lesson that is studied only once will soon be forgotten. What is repeatedly reviewed will become part of the equipment of knowledge and be permanently remembered and used. This is the real measure of achievement.

Apply and Practice Knowledge

Frequent, thorough review renders knowledge readily useful. The Scripture texts which help us most are those which have been applied and used. These verses are remembered when occasion demands. Truths which have become familiar by repetition shape conduct and mold character. If we desire to have great truths sustain and control us, we must practice them until they become habitually fixed in our lives. The "line upon line and precept upon precept" rule of the Bible is a recognition of this truth.

Review is important, necessary activity; it is an essential condition of all true teaching. Not to review is to leave teaching incomplete.

SUMMARY

Effective teaching is governed by laws of teaching and learning. These are amply illustrated in the teaching methods of Jesus.

A teacher must know his material in order to be able to teach. To communicate this knowledge, language used by the teacher must be understood by the pupil. New ideas should be introduced in terms of what the pupil already knows.

Learning, however, is done by the pupil. No learning can be accomplished unless his interest and attention are maintained. The pupil must be led to grasp the truth that is presented. As he thinks ideas into his own understanding and develops new behavior patterns, genuine learning takes place. The degree of learning can be determined and strengthened through meaningful review.

The success of teaching will be found in the diligent application of these laws.

NOTES

1. Colossians 1:16, 17
2. Colossians 2:3
3. John Milton Gregory, *The Seven Laws of Teaching* (Grand Rapids, Mich.: Baker Book House, 1954), p. viii.
4. *Ibid.*, pp. 5-7.
5. *Ibid.*, p. 6.
7. *Ibid.*
8. *Ibid.*, pp. 51-53.
9. *Ibid.*, p. 6.
10. Cecil DeBoer, *Responsible Protestantism: The Christian's Role in a Secular Society* (Grand Rapids: Wm. B. Eerdmans Pub. Co., 1957), p. 230.
11. Gregory, pp. 6, 7.
12. H. W. Dodds, *Public Schools in Crisis,* ed. Mortimer Smith (Chicago: Regnery Co., 1956), p. 67.
13. Gregory, p. 7.
14. II Timothy 4:7.
15. Gregory, p. 7.

THINK

1. How can teachers be assured of success in teaching?
2. What is the law of the teacher?
3. What is the quickest route to motivated learning?
4. In what six ways can the teacher observe the law of the language?
5. Illustrate Christ's use of the law of the lesson.
6. In what ways does a good teacher advance self-learning among his pupils?
7. Why is satisfaction important in learning?
8. Define the law of review and application.

TALK

1. Discuss to what degree each law of teaching has been observed in the class sessions thus far. Provide specific illustrations.
2. Endeavor to give examples of how each law of teaching was used by Christ in His teaching ministry.

ACT

1. During the week keep a record of the laws of teaching you use in daily communication. Make a notation as you recognize your use of a law.
2. Select any lesson for an age group in which you are interested. Show how you would use each law of teaching in presenting the lesson.

CHAPTER FIVE

INSTRUCTIONAL AIDS

Instructional aids often are the plus which leads to successful teaching.

An instructional aid is a means for improving instruction, not a crutch upon which to lean. It is "any device that assists an instructor to transmit to a learner facts, skills, attitudes, knowledge, understanding, and appreciation."[1]

IMPRESSIONAL AIDS

Teaching aids help a teacher overcome barriers to communication. The language barrier is overcome with the use of pictures, objects, and other resources for transmitting understanding and meaning. Aids also help make learning interesting by adding variety, participation, and incentive. Through the use of aids learning is more rapid and more permanent. As teachers use instructional aids effectively, student learning increases.

Impressional aids are those used in creating an impression on the student in the teaching process. These include audio devices; visuals, both projected and non-projected; and audiovisuals which utilize both sound and sight.

Audios

Sound is vital to communication and sound equipment, such as phonographs, radios, and cassette tape recorder/players, can be profitably used in church education. Probably the most adaptable for class use is the cassette player. Besides individualized study programs, the cassette player can provide the class with a panel of experts previously recorded by the teacher, music with which to sing, or the voice of the teacher presenting a lesson during a needed absence.

Visuals

Visuals can be seen but not heard. However, many visuals are combined with audio presentations to enable both the eye and ear to be used and learning increased. One value of visuals is that pupils who fail to grasp a truth through the ear gate may comprehend it through the eye.

A wide selection of visuals is available. Teachers who use them report increased interest, more constant attention, and enthusiastic response.

Visuals usually are divided into two categories—projected and non-projected. Projected aids make use of mechanical equipment such as a projector. Non-projected aids do not need such equipment.

PROJECTED VISUALS

Years ago David Livingstone used a "magic lantern" to gain interest and friendship among the African natives. Modern slide, motion picture, opaque, and overhead projectors are much advanced over Livingstone's lantern. Projectors, either with or without sound, are widely used in Christian education today.

Slides, transparencies, filmstrips, or motion pictures often are available for rent as well as purchase. This enables wide usage without large financial investment.

Careful previewing of projected visuals will enable a teacher to relate the material to the lesson emphasis.

NON-PROJECTED VISUALS

Included in this category are objects, maps, pictures, chalkboards and flipcharts, flannelgraph.

Objects are tangible items used to help define spiritual truth. Objects appeal to everybody. A small object such as a coin, stone, or paper is easily used. A scroll, for instance, will visualize the form in which the Old Testament was originally written. A homemade model of stocks will portray vividly the painful torture of Paul and Silas in prison.[2] One teacher, while telling the story of Mary anointing the Lord in Bethany, took a bottle of perfume and poured some on her handkerchief until the room was filled with the odor.[3] Another teacher, while discussing the fig tree in Mark 11, brought a fig to his class.

These are valuable and effective teaching aids. They give the pupil firsthand experience with the subject being discussed. A well-equipped church should have a collection of Bible models and missionary curios among its materials. However, any teacher can find teaching aids in the commonplace objects that are all around.

Pupils need to be familiar with Bible geography and history. *Maps* help them learn the topography and locations of Bible countries and cities. The journeys of the patriarchs, the wanderings of Israel, or the campaigns of Joshua and David cannot be followed without the use of maps. They should be consulted frequently. Small maps, conveniently located in most Bibles, are helpful. Wall maps are more practical and profitable, especially if constructed by class members. Good maps also are available on overhead transparencies. A globe, for locating mission fields and comparing the size and location of Bible lands with the pupils' own country, also is useful.

Skillful use of *pictures* results in successful instruction. Teaching can be more effective with pictures than by words alone. Some of the great works of art depict Bible scenes. If copies of the masterpieces are available, these can be used in class sessions. Often a series of pictures can be arranged to present a running narrative of the life of Christ or other Bible character.

Pupils may need help in interpreting a picture's message and its relationship to the lesson emphasis. Too much attention to details of a picture will cause the pupils to remember it more than the lesson.

Pictures are so readily available that teachers should use them freely. The Christian teacher can develop a file of good pictures collected from various sources or purchase lesson-related pictures from curriculum publishers.

Chalkboards and flipcharts are widely accepted as effective teaching aids. Every classroom should have one or the other for use by teacher and pupils. These are used to clarify the instruction by means of diagrams, outlines, and drawings presented step by step. Even the action of the teacher while using a chalkboard helps sustain attention.

It is not necessary to be a professional artist to make good use of a chalkboard or flipchart. A short line, a few stick figures, a circle, or square can represent people, cities, or events. New and difficult words, names of characters, important dates, an outline or summary can be written for class members to see. Six things to remember when using a chalkboard or flipchart are:

Avoid too much detail.
Don't block the view.
Write legibly, but quickly.
Stand at the side of your work as much as possible.
Talk while writing, but do not talk to the board.
Use chart and graph presentations whenever possible.

The *flannelgraph* is a versatile teaching device. It has been widely used in the Sunday school, vacation Bible School, children's meetings, and weekday classes.

It secures attention at the very outset and, as new factors appear, it sustains interest. At the end of the lesson, the class may repeat the story, placing the figures upon the board. This combines the faculties of hearing, seeing, and doing.

Frank G. Coleman, in *The Romance of Winning Children*, says there are three basics which must be mastered if the flannelgraph is to be used successfully—dexterity, suspense, movement.

Dexterity. The skillful manipulation of the flannelgraph is attention getting. This takes practice. The teacher should know the story and should practice telling it with the use of the flannelgraph. Everything must be ready before the class session. The figures should be arranged in the order in which they are to be used. Keep the hands as free as possible. Let the story move rapidly. Talk while you work, but keep an eye contact with the class.

Suspense. Curiosity is an important factor. Arouse pupil attention by the manner in which the figures are placed on the board. Keep the class in suspense. Hold attention until the last word has been spoken and the final figure is placed on the board. Do not place any material, except the background, on the board before you begin to speak. Develop the scene as you unfold the story and delay the final scene until the last possible moment.

Movement. If the teacher walks about as he tells the story with the flannelgraph, his movement will help to sustain attention. Every motion or gesture occupies the eye, and even though many may seem unnecessary, they will put life into the instruction.[4]

Audiovisuals

Often audio aids and visual aids are combined to assist instruction. Sound motion pictures and filmstrips are the most common of these. A teacher may produce his own unique presentation of a topic through the use of a tape and slides.

EXPRESSIONAL AIDS

A distinction can be made between aids for impression and aids for expression. Impression is related to the teaching process. It involves all the teacher does to stimulate the pupil to mental activity. Expression involves the learning process and requires the pupil to reproduce in expression the lesson he is learning—thinking it out in its various phases and applications till he can express it in his own language and behavior. The manner in which these activities of expression are employed is important in their utilization toward learning. Expressional activities provide means for appraising true learning. Christ's words, "Ye shall know them by their fruits,"[5] might well be interpreted to include the pupil's activities in times of expressional opportunities.

To be effective, the teacher must provide expressional activities that involve careful thinking, reasoning, analyzing, evaluating, summarizing. This active involvement of the mind, heart, and will urges the students to become "doers of the word."[6]

Expressional activities are part of good teaching. They are effective because they supplement the personality and skill of the instructor, and they assist the pupil in learning.

Importance

Impressional aids help to reach and stimulate the pupil's mind but they do not necessarily secure a response. Expressional aids are needed and are important for they deepen impression, capitalize on energy, and reach the personality.

DEEPEN IMPRESSION

A child will often forget what he hears; he may forget what he has seen, but he will not soon forget what he has done. Learning is a process of listening, looking, and doing. As a pupil expresses himself, he reimpresses his own mind and learns the truth through a different sense channel—not only through sight and sound, but now through activity. Learning begins and continues in what the learner does. The pupil taking piano lessons receives certain impressions when the teacher demonstrates a musical selection, but he doesn't begin to learn until he practices it for himself.

CAPITALIZE ON ENERGY

A good solution for discipline problems is keeping the active pupil occupied. His boundless energy and ceaseless activity need to be utilized. The teacher guides it, but does not try to suppress it. Directed expressional activity capitalizes on energy as it serves excellent educational purposes.

REACH THE PERSONALITY

To reach the personality, expressional aids must do more than provide busy work for restless pupils. The activities should have a positive value in shaping life. The teacher has not actually reached the personality until there has been the appropriation and application of knowledge. The aim is the development of Christian character and living. The teacher himself serves as the best visual aid. The pupils see in his life the ideal that they may attain. Unconsciously they imitate and then express similar character.

Pupil's Manual

The pupil's manual is an important expressional aid. It represents and sets the pace for the pupil's response to instruction. The manual is only a means to an end and not an end in itself. The teacher whose primary concern is that his class should show neat, orderly manuals is defeating his ultimate purpose.

With older children, it is preferable that the pupil's manual be studied and completed at home. On this foundation, the teacher can build an educational superstructure. The good teacher solicits the cooperation of the home, without which there will be little or no preparation.

Under certain circumstances, part of the class period may be used for supervised study. Written work provided in the book can be done at this time. Many teachers use this method with splendid results. They observe the pedagogical principle that teaching is getting a response.

For children above kindergarten age, every pupil's manual should include:

SOMETHING TO WRITE

There may be blanks to fill in, sentences to complete. Additional creative writing helps the pupil to record his knowledge and provides for a personal response to instruction.

SOMETHING TO FIND

The pupil who is required to search the Bible for an answer will be likely to remember the information. His activity will make an impression upon his personality and develop his initiative for the discovery of truth.

SOMETHING TO DRAW

The lesson will be strengthened if the pupil draws a map, chart, graph, or picture. This drawing need not be artistically correct or complete.

A map of Palestine may show the boundaries, Mediterranean Sea, Sea of Galilee, Jordan River, and Dead Sea. The pupil can locate and print the names of several important cities. These are the basic geographical factors for a study of the life of Christ. Other items can be added as the story develops.

SOMETHING TO APPLY

The search for knowledge and understanding has reached its goal when the pupil is able to transfer new ideas into the experiences of his own life.

Handcraft

Years ago Marion Lawrence stated that "a child remembers 10% of what he hears, 50% of what he sees, 70% of what he says, and 90% of what he does." What a pupil discovers and writes and draws and constructs will be indelibly impressed upon his mind. But in all probability he will best remember what he constructs.

The teaching time is too brief for extended work in manual arts. However, manual expression is more than busy work, and pupils do not waste time if the construction is correlated with instruction.

Handcraft also may be used during presession activities.

MATERIALS

Many inexpensive materials are available for handcraft projects. These include paper, pasteboard, plastic, plaster. A Bible-times village can be constructed entirely of paper, cloth, and wood.

PROJECTS

A resourceful teacher will use projects that are related to one lesson, or to a lesson series. A class will learn more by constructing a model of the tabernacle than by reading the Exodus description many times. Making a relief map of Palestine will teach more about the mountains and valleys than by reading about them, or even by special instruction in Bible geography.

Observation Trips

One of the amazing features of Jesus' teaching is that very little of it took place within the classroom. His lessons were drawn from the world around him—the fields, the birds, the flowers. Through observation trips the enterprising teacher can provide new experiences for his pupils.

Trips are both expressional and impressional. A visit to the zoo, the park, or a farm will provide many opportunities to teach the greatness of God's creation and His loving care. Pupil participation in planning and evaluation adds to the learning experience.

Careful advance planning is necessary for the observation trip. Arrangements with church leadership, selection of the destination, permission from parents, travel arrangements, and a careful discussion of the purpose of the experience are all essential. Pupils can be deeply involved at all levels and learning will be pleasant and permanent.

All these aids for expression will strengthen the spiritual life of a pupil. The teacher utilizes classroom activity as a means of making impressions vivid, permanent, vital, and appealing. Correlated expressional activities develop Christian character and Christian living.

SUMMARY

Every teacher's work can be strengthened by the use of instructional aids. They will help overcome communication barriers and enhance the speed and permanence of teaching.

Impressional aids are concerned with the law of teaching; they involve the attempt to stimulate pupil response. Audiovisuals are impressional aids.

Expressional aids include the pupil's manual, handcraft, and participation in observation trips. They involve the learning process and encourage pupil participation. Their use will deepen the teaching impression and help to effect beneficial changes in the pupil's character.

NOTES

1. Kenneth B. Haas and Harry Q. Packer, *Preparation and Use of Audio-Visual Aids* (New York: Prentice-Hall, Inc., 1950), p. xi.
2. Acts 16:24
3. John 12:1-8
4. Frank G. Coleman, *The Romance of Winning Children* (Cleveland: Union Gospel Press, 1948), p. 146.
5. Matthew 7:16
6. James 1:22

THINK

1. What are some of the values of instructional aids?
2. Define audiovisual aids.
3. Give some examples of the use of objects with a Bible lesson.
4. List several suggestions for using a chalkboard effectively.
5. State three fundamental principles for using flannelgraph.
6. Compare impressional and expressional teaching aids.
7. Name three values of expressional aids.
8. What are the values of observation trips?

TALK

1. After each group member has listed all the impressional aids available in his church, discuss a program for making these known to all teachers, instructing teachers in their use, and making them available.
2. Discuss a possible program of expressional activities for a class of junior children who wish to do something helpful for the church.

ACT

1. Visit a class and determine the proportion of class time spent with impressional teaching aids and that spent with expressional aids. Evaluate the effectiveness of this division of time.
2. Cut handcraft ideas from magazines, newspapers, and other publications. File these according to age groups with suggestions how each can be utilized as an instructional aid.

CHAPTER SIX

GATHERING LESSON MATERIAL

Lesson material is to be found everywhere but must be gathered when available.

Today's church needs trained teachers who put their whole mind into their preparation, their whole heart into their presentation, and their whole life into their illustration. A trained teacher knows that he needs preparation. Poise cannot be maintained in the presence of a class without mastery of the lesson and a reserve knowledge of Bible truth. Full preparedness calls for definite plans and definite plans include properly selected materials.

SOURCES OF MATERIAL

The capable teacher uses materials from many sources to develop his lesson.

Bible

The Bible is the teacher's major source of material, his primary base of teaching. Because it is the inspired Word of God, it is the recognized text of the church. Every teacher must become a serious student of the Bible. He will study, interpret, digest, and apply until he masters the spirit of the message and absorbs the Word in his life.

The Bible is its own best interpreter. A comparison of Scriptures with Scriptures will throw light on obscure passages. Also there are many valuable supplementary materials that help the Bible teacher to master the Word of God.

INFORMATION

Some Bibles contain valuable notes and geographical, historical, and archaeological helps. More complete helps may also be purchased in separate volumes. The E.T.T.A. bibliography, *Books For Christian Educators,* provides helpful information and lists many suggested books.

INTERPRETATION

Some Bibles have notes and comments on various passages. In this arrangement a commentary is provided with the text. These explanations have especial value to teachers who do not have specialized training.

INVESTIGATION

Good teachers help their pupils become independent investigators. This is impossible unless the teacher develops his own abilities and techniques of investigation. A reference Bible will help both teacher and pupil locate parallel passages and other information that illustrates the truth being studied.

Bible Dictionary

A Bible dictionary seeks to provide meaning and understanding of events, persons, places, and words used in the Bible.

Bible Concordance

An exhaustive concordance lists all the major biblical references for the individual words in the Bible and may also give meanings and related information. Strong's, Cruden's, and Young's complete concordances are widely accepted.

Bible Commentary

After a careful and prayerful investigation of the Scriptures, the teacher may consult Bible commentaries for interpretations of difficult passages. Reliable, up-to-date commentaries are written by recognized Bible scholars who are abreast of recent developments in biblical literature and archaeology. These volumes should be available in every church library. Commentaries, however, should not be accepted as the final, complete answer. Commentators may vary in their opinions. The use of several reliable commentaries will provide a cross section of interpretation.

Teacher's Manual

In studying his lesson, the teacher reads the Bible, first for the story; then for the incidents; next for the persons mentioned; then for its doctrinal and practical teachings; and finally for the spirit of the message. After a background of independent study, the teacher consults manuals and other lesson helps. By following this order, he personally discovers many facts mentioned in the lesson helps and has the satisfaction of blazing the trail for himself.

The teacher's manual should supplement the teacher's knowledge. It should be used with the Bible, never as a substitute for it. Any teacher who uses a teacher's manual without first studying the Bible passage independently is apt to do little original thinking or teaching.

Lesson helps can clarify difficult passages, provide apt illustrations, and supply essential information on ancient manners and customs. The teacher should use Bible-centered, Christ-honoring lesson helps so that he may obtain a right understanding, interpretation, and application of the Scripture.

The teacher's manual is a valuable asset for it provides Bible lesson material and information for understanding the relation of this material to the age group to be taught.

BIBLE LESSON MATERIAL

The teacher's manual can be a source of profitable Bible study directly related to the lesson. Although the teacher's manual should be studied, it is not necessary to limit instruction to its contents. Evangelical literature for the church educational program usually contains good biblical reference material to give the teacher a broad basis for understanding the lesson content.

AGE GROUP EMPHASIS

Ministering to pupils means meeting their deepest needs. The manual can help the teacher to understand his pupils and age group in which they are and see how Bible knowledge can meet present-day living problems. Often in the manual, problems similar to those in a particular class will be suggested. So the lesson can be adapted to an immediate recognized need.

A prepared teacher does not need his manual during the class period. By teaching from the Bible, he reminds his pupils of the inspired source of Christian instruction. His attitude toward the Bible is his strongest means of non-verbal communication of its worth.

Current Sources

There are innumerable sources for enriching lessons: life experiences of teacher and pupils; current events in magazines, newspapers, bulletins, radio, and television. Schools, colleges, and government agencies often have audiovisual lending libraries. Manufacturers and distributors offer valuable audiovisual literature and catalogs, often free of charge. The local library, travel agency, or the government can furnish vital information.

The teacher who is up to date on current affairs, who knows his subject thoroughly, and who understands his pupils will teach from the overflow of his rich life. Being resourceful, he will encourage resourcefulness in his pupils.

SELECTING MATERIAL

The teacher, like a newspaper reporter, should be on the alert for material. In his devotional study; in his reading of books, magazines, and newspapers; in listening to the radio and television; and in every personal contact he should be gathering material for long-range lesson preparation.

Plan for Future Lessons

In carefully planned curriculums, each lesson is related to those preceding and those following. Taken together, they develop a complete theme. Each study must be related to the general theme for the entire unit.

To assure full, active class participation the teacher must make assignments in advance of the lesson. This cannot be done unless the teacher has given considerable time to long-range planning and study. Consideration of future lessons is both practical and essential if the teacher is to have an effective ministry.

Provide for Needs of Individual Pupils

As materials are selected, the teacher should be aware of the needs of the entire class. He should also keep a clear focus on individual members and be alert for materials to meet the needs of each pupil. This will enrich each lesson and each pupil.

Meet Personal Needs of the Teacher

The trained, consecrated teacher realizes the importance of reading selectively, systematically, and intelligently. He knows that he can help his pupils only in the proportion that he is tapping reservoirs to enrich his own spiritual growth. As he extends his own vision, increases his own knowledge, deepens his own spirituality, and vitalizes his own faith, his pupils will drink from rivers of living water rather than stagnant pools.

In addition to a systematic Bible study, the teacher will constantly seek to enrich his life by a planned reading program. This will include biographies, history, novels, and interpretations of present social trends.

ACCUMULATING MATERIAL

Some claim that 90 percent of the ideas entering the mind are soon forgotten. One eminent educator believes that most ideas are lost in the first 24 hours. Provision should therefore be made for gathering and conserving worthwhile materials.

Paint Mental Pictures

The teacher who can present facts vividly will appeal to the imagination of his pupils. But he cannot show his pupils what he himself does not see. For this reason, lesson material should be reproduced in mental pictures. During his preparation, the teacher should occasionally close his eyes and form vivid pictures of the scenes and persons about whom he has been reading. This will develop his ability to visualize and will make his teaching more creative.

Provide a Notebook

Writing helps the memory retain information and preserves it for future use. Recording and filing materials make them available at a later time. Such a depository of teaching materials will be increasingly helpful.

FOR GENERAL INFORMATION

Never read without thinking; never think without writing. The teacher who finds something worthwhile should copy it into his notebook or make a notation of the subject, book, and page, so that it can be quickly located when needed. The notebook should also include facts, experiences, and illustrations.

Facts and statistics are valuable. They form a foundation and a strong resource for class discussion. Quotations from representatives leaders and educators carry authority. Information about the latest discoveries and inventions is useful as a point of contact with a wide-awake class.

Personal experiences and human interest stories are fascinating. Many are related to the spiritual realm; answers to prayer; reports of God's providence; demonstrations of God's power; missionary adventure. These are most effective if they are related to some class member or generally known as current news events. All pertinent information should be recorded correctly, including names, dates, places, sources of information.

Teachers also need a large fund of stories and other illustrative material. Daily living is full of illustrations, but unless notes are made at the time, they will soon be forgotten. By taking notes and referring to them during lesson preparation, it is possible to have current, captivating illustrations for every lesson.

FOR SPECIFIC LESSONS

The teacher's notebook is valuable in planning for future lessons. The teacher can survey the entire lesson series and strengthen each lesson. If he faithfully uses his notebook, he will soon come to regard it as one of his chief pedagogical aids.

It is helpful to have a notebook with at least one page for each lesson of the coming quarter. Some suggest a notebook covering an entire year. Each page could indicate the lesson title and Scripture reference. As the teacher observes or discovers illustrative material, he could copy it on the appropriate page and thereby store up good teaching material for the future.

Build a File

Starting a file is easy. It will enrich every teaching experience. Materials can be accumulated for use in the months and years to come. Seasonal themes can be highlighted—Christmas, Thanksgiving, Easter. Pictures, object lessons, and other visual aids can be added. Assembling and filing material can mean real success in teaching and learning.

SUMMARY

Gathering lesson materials is a challenging and rewarding experience. The teacher must constantly be on the alert for material which will enhance his teaching. The Bible and related Bible study aids should always be near at hand as they are his basic study tools.

Selection of material is effective when it becomes a systematic, planned process with future lessons, pupil, and teacher needs in mind. Where material is carefully accumulated and wisely used, it greatly enriches the work of the teacher.

THINK

1. Name and evaluate at least seven sources of lesson material.
2. What types of supplementary helps do some Bibles have?
3. Outline a good procedure for studying the Bible lesson.
4. Why should lesson helps be used?
5. What caution should be exercised in the use of lesson helps?
6. Why are needs of individual students to be considered in the selection of material?
7. Why must the heart and mind of the teacher be prepared?
8. What are the values of using a notebook for general and specific information?

TALK

1. Discuss the importance of each of a number of sources of lesson materials provided by the teacher. Endeavor to determine their relative value by selecting one at a time according to its importance.
2. Discuss the particular contribution of a teacher's manual in gathering lesson materials. Illustrate by copies of teacher's manuals various members have brought.

ACT

1. Prepare a notebook as suggested in this chapter. Record the lesson titles for at least 13 consecutive lessons at the top of 13 separate pages. Write as many suggestions as you can for each lesson.
2. Collect informational and inspirational material and classify it according to subject matter and age level. Include pictures, poems, articles, and statistics for several age groups.

CHAPTER SEVEN

ORGANIZING THE LESSON

An organized lesson results in organized presentation.

Lesson material needs organization. This requires elimination as well as accumulation. A teacher may not teach every detail of an assigned lesson, but he should endeavor to complete all that he planned. Well-organized, carefully-outlined material will fit into the lesson period so that the entire time will be used to the best advantage.

WAYS TO ORGANIZE A LESSON

There are various ways to organize material for effective presentation. It can be assembled in a logical, chronological, or psychological manner.

Logical

This consists of sorting and selecting relevant material. Different parts are fitted together logically—proceeding from the known to the unknown. This produces logical thinking on the part of the teacher and his pupils and helps clarify truths to be learned.

Chronological

Large portions of the Bible can best be grasped and retained when presented in their historical relationship. God's revelation to man was chronological. In each age He revealed more of His divine purpose to chosen writers who spoke as they were moved by the Holy Spirit.[1] Chronological organization is related to the preparation of each lesson and to the entire curriculum of Bible study.

Psychological

This method consists of planning the subject matter to fit the comprehension and experience of the pupil. There is little purpose in teaching truth, however significant and profound, which is beyond the comprehension of the pupil. Material must be adapted to the understanding or it is soon forgotten. Even if retained, it will be dull and uninteresting.

Both secular and Christian educators stress the psychological organization of materials. However, this method must not be permitted to deemphasize the Bible content of instruction. There must be a balanced emphasis on both the application and the acquisition of God's Word. It is true that we dare not forget the pupil when we teach. It is equally true that we dare not forget the Bible— the only authoritative revelation of the truths of Christianity. Bible-centered material can be presented with an awareness of the age and understanding of the pupil.

The kindergartener requires materials and methods that differ from those required by the high school student. The junior has different needs than the adult. In each case the Bible is the source for the material, but the adaptation of the material is geared to the age group and its developmental needs.

STEPS IN ORGANIZING A LESSON

A well-organized lesson is the result of several important steps. These begin with a teacher's objective consideration of what should be emphasized and lead to the application of these emphases in the learners' lives.

Determine Emphases

Lesson emphases are based on a clear concept of the central truth in the Bible passage or passages presented in the lesson and the meaning of the passage in the lives of class members.

CENTRAL TRUTH

Every lesson contains much more than can be taught during the allotted period. Therefore, the teacher must identify and concentrate on the central truth of the Scripture passage. A thorough study of the passage, the lesson title, the memory selection, and the outline of the lesson will help determine the major emphasis.

AIM OF INSTRUCTION

All preparation will center around the aim or purpose of the lesson. Curriculum materials should be examined in the light of this purpose. The teacher should ask himself: "What can I find here to meet the need of my class members?"

The teacher's lesson manual will probably suggest a general aim for the series and specific aims for individual lessons. The teacher, however, is not limited to these aims. He must adapt the lesson aims to the needs of the class he is teaching.

Does the lesson teach faith, obedience, love, duty to God and man? Does it stress the Christian graces of humility, kindness, generosity? Is Bible study, prayer, Christian fellowship encouraged? Does it present and explain the call of God for Christian service at home or abroad? Does it deal with the gospel—God's plan of salvation? The teacher should constantly direct these truths to reach and affect each member of the class. He should be constantly aware of individual needs. Specializing in the individual will help provide dynamic motivation for selecting the methods and materials he uses.

Select Methods and Materials

To allow for preparation both methods and materials should be selected well in advance of class presentation.

METHODS

Many factors are involved in determining the methods to be used. These include the pupils' ages and the lesson content. A good teacher will vary his methods for more effective presentation. More content material is needed for a lecture than for discussion. More time is required for student reports and assignments. If questions are to be used extensively, less content material can be covered.

The character of the lesson will also determine its treatment. For example, the conquests of Joshua or the journeys of Paul will require extensive visual instruction.

MATERIALS

After deciding the aim and method, the teacher should study all the available helps. Not all lesson helps can be used. The teacher must select those which will help in the realization of his aim. After years of teaching experience one teacher wrote: "If I had to do it over, I would think less of what I was giving, and more of what the pupils were getting."

Reports, assignments, questions, Bible memory work, pictures, and other collateral material require lesson time. However, all these materials contribute to well-rounded lesson development.

Plan the Lesson

A lesson plan should be brief, simple, and practical. It will aid the teacher in directing and organizing his lesson. Preparing a good lesson plan will actually conserve time and effort.

Following is a suggested lesson plan. The steps necessary to a teacher's preparation have been summarized and placed in this outline. However, the teacher may adapt this plan to his specific needs.

Lesson title
Scripture
Memory verse
Central truth
Lesson aim
Lesson outline

> Approach (create a readiness for learning)
> Body (include a selection of teaching methods, audio-
>   visuals, questions, and illustrations)
> Conclusion (apply the lesson to life)
> Possible assignments for the following lesson
> Evaluation of the class session (to be filled in after the lesson
>   has been taught)

Trained, experienced teachers often prepare their own outlines of material and procedure. Inexperienced teachers may prefer to use outlines suggested in a teacher's manual. With study and experience, however, all teachers can soon learn to construct their own outlines and lesson plans.

The ease, effectiveness, and conclusiveness with which the lesson is taught depends largely on the clarity of the outline. Facts should be listed in the order of their importance under the topic or division to which they are related. The teacher can easily prearrange the climax so that it comes in the concluding minutes. If there is insufficient time for every detail, he can cover the main heads of the outline, omitting some secondary topics. Following this plan, the teacher will be certain of enough time to complete the lesson.

Relate to Life

Little is gained from teaching if it does not relate to life. A well-organized lesson often incorporates questions, illustrations, and planned application which direct the pupils' thoughts to the meaning of the lesson for their personal lives.

QUESTIONS

If the lesson is to be developed by the use of questions, the facts and truths should be brought into prominence so that the pupils will recognize the train of thought, and feel that they are making progress as the lesson proceeds.

The teacher can inspire good participation by thoughtful questions. Advance preparation of these makes it easier to formulate specific, thought-provoking questions that are pertinent to the lesson. However, the best questions often result from the response of the pupils and therefore cannot be completely anticipated in advance.

ILLUSTRATIONS

Appropriate illustrations must be selected beforehand and included in the outline. Some teachers introduce the lesson with an illustration. This approach gains attention and sets the stage for the presentation. The opening illustration may be woven into the entire teaching period and regiven at its close. It is a rewarding experience to anticipate points that will need clarification and then to illustrate them from everyday experience such as nature, history, stories, or songs.

APPLICATION

This important phase of preparation is not difficult for the teacher who has assembled and organized his material to meet the pupils' needs. Every teacher should ask himself this pertinent question. "How can I get my class to express in daily living the truths that I am preparing to teach?" The Holy Spirit will enable the teacher to follow the right procedure as he prays and plans for the personal application.

Involve Pupils

Involving pupils requires careful thought. Teaching is more inclusive than simply lecturing. The best teachers guide their pupils to become independent investigators of truth. Definite assignments for each learner should be planned in advance. The desire for pupil cooperation will motivate the teacher to plan and involve students through research projects and class reports.

RESEARCH PROJECTS

Research assignments may be made for the individual or group. They may be done as lesson preparation or by the group during the class session. In either case, assignments should be definite and individual.

It is not enough to urge pupils to study the lesson and complete projects. Even those who want to do this may be overwhelmed and discouraged by the bigness of the task. The teacher must communicate clearly, helping pupils know how to study and what to study.

It is also essential that the teacher suggest definite sources of help. Without proper guidance, pupils will not know what books to consult. Usually it is advisable to give them the material and offer to help them in research.

Assignments should be personal and individual. One pupil may be given a question to answer; another, a topic for study and report; a third, a map to draw; a fourth, some Bible references to compare. The interest, capacity, and ability of each class member should be considered in selecting the nature of the assignment. Whenever possible, every member of the class should be included.

CLASS REPORTS

Pupils are frustrated if they do out-of-class assignments and then are not given opportunity to report their findings in class.

A good teacher plans for the presentation of all assignments, using various means to make these effective. This requires making assignments sufficiently in advance.

The teacher who knows the interests of the pupils plans questions which encourage them to express themselves freely.

If the class has a good background of Bible knowledge or is making an intensive or extensive study of the lesson, individual pupils may use their assigned topics to introduce general discussion. Members of the class will usually participate in any discussion they introduce. Failure to secure initial involvement may hinder full cooperation. Under the skillful leadership of a trained teacher, even the timid and the slow learner can be drawn into class activities.

STUDENT TEACHING

In classes for older youth and adults, it is sometimes profitable to have one of the students teach the lesson. This experience for the student teacher should be carefully supervised, so that each class member will have a genuine learning experience. The teacher should brief the student teacher before the class session. During a post-session evaluation the student teacher may be encouraged to pursue training courses and thus qualify for future teaching.

SUMMARY

Successful teaching requires the careful organization of material according to a clear lesson plan. The central truth of the lesson and the needs of the class members will provide the basis for selecting an aim. The lesson outline is then developed which will achieve the aim most effectively. Of particular significance is the involvement of the student in the teaching experience.

NOTES

1. II Peter 1:21

THINK

1. What is the value of a well-organized lesson?
2. What are three methods of organizing material?
3. Describe the steps in organizing material.
4. How is the central truth determined?
5. What factors determine the methods to be used?
6. How does one determine the amount of material to be used?
7. Discuss the outline of a good lesson plan.
8. What plans should be made to involve all pupils in class participation?

TALK

1. What is the comparative importance of the various sections of a lesson plan? Discuss proportionate time allotments in preparation and in presentation.
2. Discuss the possible values and problems of writing a lesson in advance of presentation.

ACT

1. Ask several teachers to give you the lesson outline they used in teaching a recent lesson. Endeavor to determine what portions had been especially well prepared and how detailed the outline was.
2. Without the help of a lesson manual select an appropriate portion of Scripture and prepare a lesson plan for teaching the age group in which you are primarily interested.

CHAPTER EIGHT

QUESTIONS AND ILLUSTRATIONS

Questions and illustrations are doors and windows for increased enlightenment.

Questions and illustrations vitalize Christian teaching and lead to better pupil understanding and spiritual growth.

ASKING QUESTIONS

The question is a teaching device that can be both powerful and effective. Asking questions is a skill which, when acquired, is a great asset to a teacher. The interrogation point is thought by some to be the badge of the teaching profession. Francis Bacon declared that "the skillful question is the half of knowledge." The real test of a teacher is the response of his pupils. His questions must not only instruct, but educate—lead out his pupils. The response will depend on the skill with which the question is used.

The Gospel accounts record more than one hundred startling, unusual, unexpected questions. The Lord Jesus Christ was a master of the art of questioning. At the age of twelve He was asking questions.[1] At the beginning of His public ministry He asked His first two disciples, "What seek ye?" This is typical of the thought-provoking and reflecting character of all His questions. Even in His preaching He frequently asked, "What think ye?" and "How think ye?" A study of our Lord's questions is in itself a course in teaching techniques.

Why Ask Questions

To appreciate the value of good questions, the teacher must understand their purpose. Questions provide an important stimulus to the mind. The question serves many purposes.

To Awaken Interest

The teacher must make contact with pupils in order to arouse their interest. A question, carefully worded to strike the mind, is like a fisherman's bait on a hook. It catches the interest and elicits immediate, spontaneous response. It stimulates the pupil's thinking and focuses his immediate interest on the lesson.

To Direct Thought

After contact has been established, each succeeding question should move toward the teacher's goal. Stimulated by questions that have unity and purpose, learners can be directed from one area of thought to another.

To Quicken Participation

When a pupil's mind has wandered, it can be recalled by a question. In an atmosphere of dullness, thinking becomes sluggish. A well-aimed series of questions will put new life into class. Questions with life and vivacity will assure satisfactory progress.

To Drive Home the Truth

Pupils may discuss a Bible truth without associating it in any way with themselves. A good question will lead them to apply the truth to their own lives. Christ illustrated this when He asked His disciples, "Whom do men say that I the Son of man am?" When they responded, He quickly applied their thought by the personal question, "But whom say ye that I am?"[2]

Preparation of Questions

Good teachers prepare their questions in advance. Several different types should be studied and used.

Contact Questions

Attention and interest can be aroused if the teacher begins the lesson with an appropriate contact question. The most familiar and frequent expression of Jesus was, "What think ye?" Conversations were introduced by inquiries such as, "Will ye also go away?", "Whereupon shall we liken the kingdom of God?", and "Whence shall we buy bread that these may eat?"

Rhetorical Questions

Preachers and teachers often ask questions without expecting an answer. Such inquiries are asked for effect rather than reply. They occasion surprise and issue vital challenges; they stimulate mental activity.

Study the questions in the Sermon on the Mount in Matthew, chapters 6 and 7. "Which of you by taking thought can add one cubit unto his stature?" "Why take ye thought for raiment?" "Why beholdest thou the mote that is in thy brother's eye?" "Do men gather grapes of thorns, or figs of thistles?" Such questions do not demand answers. They require action.

Factual Questions

The easiest questions are those that can be answered by information previously given. The reply fixes in the mind the instruction that has already been imparted, and, since the work of a teacher is not complete until it has been tested, factual questions reveal how much instruction has reached its goal. A good teacher is concerned that his pupils have many opportunities to reproduce the lessons they have learned.

Thought-Provoking Questions

Questions must do more than test the pupil's knowledge. They also must help him organize and apply his knowledge. They should stimulate the pupil to study more and to think for himself.

A good teacher in order to stimulate his pupils will use questions not only to direct thought, but to provoke thought as well. He will prepare thought-provoking questions that involve purpose, opinion, and application.

The word *what* elicits information; *why* determines purpose. A direct appeal to the reasoning abilities of a student will encourage independent thought. Our Lord demonstrated this approach many times. For instance, He struck at the consciences of His critics when He asked, "Is it lawful to do good on the sabbath day, or to do evil? to save life, or to kill?"[3] "Why call ye me, Lord, Lord, and do not the things which I say?"[4]

Questions calling for personal judgment usually are more valuable than those that ask for statement of fact. Pupils must learn to determine relative values. Personal judgment was encouraged by our Lord's questions, "What thinkest thou, Simon?"[5] and "Why callest thou me good?"[6] Many of His questions were used to strengthen faith, "Wilt thou be made whole?"[7]; "Believe ye that I am able to do this?"[8]; "Whosoever liveth and believeth in me shall never die. Believest thou this?"[9]

The most thought-provoking question leads to a practical, personal application of truth. A lawyer seeking a debate raised the question, "Who is my neighbour?"[10] Christ answered with the story of the Good Samaritan and asked the lawyer's opinion as to which of the three strangers was a true neighbor. The lawyer's reply called forth the divine dictum, "Go and do thou likewise." In an entirely different situation Christ asked Peter the heart-searching question, "Lovest thou me?" and followed it by the command, "Feed my lambs."[11]

How to Ask Questions

The successful use of questions depends largely upon the way they are asked. The observance of the following principles will enrich the teacher, make his teachings more effective, and encourage class members.

Do not read questions.
Avoid questions that reveal the answers.
Avoid guessing questions which can be answered yes or no.
Avoid long questions or double questions.
Ask definite questions.

Do not repeat questions and answers.
State questions before assigning.
Assign questions judiciously.
Encourage questions.
Answer questions with questions.

Teachers usually ask questions to find out the extent of the pupils' knowledge. Pupils ask questions because they face difficulties which they wish to clarify. An effective teaching procedure is to present a problem and challenge the class in the form of a question needing an answer. This is better than presenting the solution and then testing afterward to see if the class understands it. The wise teacher constantly stimulates the spirit of inquiry. He does not tell his class something they can find out for themselves. To help them do this he encourages questions from class members and often answers questions with other questions.

EFFECTIVE ILLUSTRATIONS

A skillful teacher also knows how to use one of the most valuable implements of instruction—the illustration. The illustration is a reference to familiar ground. It constitutes an important application of the law that the pupil learns the new in terms of the old.

Values of Illustrations

All teachers should realize the effectiveness of illustrations and cultivate the skillful use of them. The teacher's work is not done when he has presented the facts of a lesson. Unless these truths are placed within his pupil's understanding little learning will take place.

The Lord Jesus Christ used many illustrations in teaching. He often said, "The kingdom of heaven is like unto. . ." He recognized that new instruction needed the illumination of the light from familiar scenes. Frequently He referred to nature and human life to clarify His instruction.

A striking object lesson was necessary before Peter could understand that God did not want Peter's old prejudices to stand in the way of his ministry to the Gentiles.[12]

The Old Testament also presents an impressive array of illustrations used by the prophets. Jeremiah used the girdle, the bottle, and the potter's vessel; Ezekiel, the roll, the tile, the beard; Amos, the locust, the plumbline, the summer fruits; Zechariah, the myrtle trees, the measuring lines, the candlestick.

Even though illustrations are important, their value is lessened if they are overdone. Sometimes a story is so vividly told that it is remembered but the truth forgotten. Striking illustrations that will recall the truth are needed.

Kinds of Illustrations

Sources of illustrations are almost unlimited. The observant teacher finds them in everything he sees or does. And there is almost no end to the ways in which they may be used in teaching. There are, however, two general divisions—visual and verbal.

Visual

Pupils receive and remember much of what is directed to the eye gate and comprehend such instruction easily and quickly.

It is one thing to use an *object* for study; it is vastly different to use it for illustration. When Christ placed a child in the center of the group, the little one did not become the subject of discussion, but the striking illustration of humility. Whenever a pupil's eye rests on some object related to the truth to be conveyed, the dubious look on his face gives way to the smile of comprehension.

When living objects are not available, *pictures* and *photographs* may be substituted. What words cannot convey, the picture may communicate.

Often *models* of the ark, the temple, and oriental houses will convey truth more readily and accurately than verbal descriptions. *Drawings* and *diagrams* also are helpful. With all age groups the teacher can use *chalkboard* or *flipchart* to advantage.

To help to visualize locations, especially in lessons that involve the movement of the characters, *maps* can be used.

Verbal

When verbal illustrations are used, they must be in clear, simple language. Words and phrases that are familiar to the hearers will help them grasp the truth.

The Bible is the best source of verbal illustrations. These stories convey the truth as God intended. Next to Bible stories, the best illustrations come from everyday life. Real life stories should be told vividly, faithfully portraying the illustrative details but not sacrificing the truth.

Parables must be distinguished from simple stories. Our Lord had a larger purpose in view by their use. Jesus seldom defined the doctrines He proclaimed. An example of this is the kingdom of heaven about which He taught so frequently. To His hearers, its deepest meaning was not fully understood. Christ did not give a formal definition. However, in Matthew 13, He did reveal its character by illustrations which were familiar to His listeners.

Jesus did not always furnish an interpretation of His parabolic teaching. For some parables He gave the key.[13] His illustrations provoked thought and aroused the spirit of inquiry which He satisfied when He was alone with the disciples.

Making *comparisons* is one of the easiest and simplest uses of illustration. As pupils grow in knowledge and experience, this method becomes proportionately successful. It is interesting to note how frequently Christ used comparisons. He declared, "I am the bread of life"; "I am the living water"; "I am the good shepherd"; "I am the vine." He called His disciples "the salt of the earth," "the light of the world."

Older students may be appealed to by *allusions* to historical, biographical, literary, and scientific data. This time-saving device provides food for thought and stimulates study in order to understand the meaning implied. The scholarly Paul used similes and metaphors to explain nearly every spiritual truth in the Christian life. Undoubtedly Paul was familiar with law, medicine, teaching, architecture, warfare, agriculture, commerce, Greek games, and seafaring life. He referred to all these in his teaching.

How to Use Illustrations

What makes an illustration vital? Why do some illustrations sparkle with interest? Why do others fall flat? It is important to understand the right use of an illustration. To be effective an illustration must have several characteristics.

BRIEF

Illustrations must be long enough to convey the truth adequately, but brief enough to allow the hearer to absorb the teaching.

NEW AND FRESH

Effective illustrations will be new and fresh. They can be drawn from current events and daily experiences. Their freshness will appeal to every alert pupil.

CLEAR

An illustration must clearly depict the meaning of the truth. It should be familiar to the hearer, drawn from the realm of his experiences.

DIGNIFIED

Illustrations should be dignified, in keeping with the level of spiritual truth. Purity of life and thought must always match purity of doctrine.

SUMMARY

The use of questions is a powerful teaching device. It was used successfully by Christ and various biblical writers. Questions will help the teacher direct the application specifically to the life of the pupil and involve him directly in the teaching process.

A teacher should be well prepared for the use of questions. He will need to be familiar with the various types and purposes of questions, as well as the principles governing their use.

Another significant method to enhance teaching is the use of illustrations. Christ's parables were striking in their effect. Some illustrations may be visual such as objects, pictures, models, or maps. Stories, parables, comparisons, and allusions belong to the verbal category. Illustrations are "windows to let in light" and should become the tool of every teacher who aspires to influence the lives of his class members.

NOTES

1. Luke 2:46
2. Matthew 16:13-15
3. Mark 3:4
4. Luke 6:46
5. Matthew 17:25
6. Matthew 19:17
7. John 5:6
8. Matthew 9:28
9. John 11:26
10. Luke 10:25-37
11. John 21:15-17
12. Acts 10:9-26
13. Matthew 13:18-23, 36-43

THINK

1. Discuss the value of good questions in the teaching-learning process.
2. List four types of questions and discuss the value and purpose of each.
3. What are the significant characteristics of thought-provoking questions?
4. List six or more principles for the successful use of questions.
5. To what important law of teaching is the illustration related?
6. Name four types of visual illustrations and state the value of each.
7. List various types of verbal illustration and their values.
8. Name five requisites for a vital illustration.

TALK

1. Read Romans 3, assigning one verse to each member in sequence. Whenever a question is reached have the reader change it to a statement. Discuss the resultant difference in learning impact.
2. Discuss one lesson illustration each group member best remembers. Endeavor to determine the lesson theme from the illustration.

ACT

1. Start a file of illustrations classified according to subject and age level. Include at least ten subjects and have at least one illustration for each age group from primaries through adults.
2. Read through the teaching ministry of Christ and find an example of each kind of question referred to in the textbook content.

CHAPTER NINE

TEACHING THE LESSON

A good lesson presentation is the fulfillment of careful planning.

Effective Christian teaching is the result of the Holy Spirit empowerment. This, however, does not eliminate the need for a practical knowledge of good teaching techniques. Spirituality and correct methodology are not mutually exclusive. Unless there has been careful, prayerful, Spirit-guided preparation, teaching is likely to be fruitless. Study is a prerequisite for effective teaching.

Training also is essential. While pursuing a training course does not guarantee that a teacher is qualified, training helps establish the basic knowledge, attitudes, and skills of the teacher.

APPROACHING THE LESSON PERIOD

If the teacher follows the steps outlined in the preceding chapters, specific preparation for any lesson will be more simple. The preparation and teaching of a lesson can be approached with confidence if the general aims, objectives, and principles of teaching are clearly understood. The resulting joy in teaching and the pupil's enthusiastic response will make this approach worthwhile.

Prepared Plans

Prayer and preparation determine whether the teaching of a lesson will be drudgery or joy. For the well-trained, carefully-prepared teacher, each lesson is a satisfying experience. Having given adequate time, prayer, and thought to planning the work, the final step for the teacher is to work the plan.

Presession Period

The campaign for attention and interest begins before the first pupil arrives. The teacher should be in the classroom early so he will be able to greet each member as he arrives. A teacher who is late is already at a disadvantage. The teacher can profitably use the time before pupils arrive to check the classroom temperature, displays, seating arrangement, and teaching materials.

INTRODUCING THE LESSON

The teacher's first sentences may determine the success or failure of the entire lesson. Upon the spirit and method of this opening depend the results that follow. The most carefully made plans avail little if the teacher fails in his approach to the lesson. The first concern is to establish right attitudes and interest among the class members.

Contact With the Class

Pupils are likely to be absorbed with interests outside the lesson. Their minds are intent on other things, so the lesson is faced with indifference.

To create readiness for learning the teacher must accomplish three things. First, he must establish a point of contact. The beginning must be on the learner's level of interest and need. Next, he must arouse interest in learning. Finally, he will focus attention on the lesson. Even the best introduction is of little avail if it does not open the door to the lesson.[1]

There are numerous ways to arouse genuine interest.

CURRENT NEWS EVENTS

The teacher may secure attention by referring to some current news. Older students read the newspapers, listen to the radio, and watch television. They have a wide range of interests. Younger children respond to any event related to their school or play. Teachers who are well informed and keenly interested in the weekday activities of the pupils have no difficulty at this point.

STORIES AND ILLUSTRATIONS

A well-told story arouses and sustains attention. A picture or an object gains immediate response. To attract attention and impress a truth upon the learners, an illustration from everyday experience is a good procedure.

REPORTS OF ASSIGNMENTS

People are interested in their own activities. Unless their homework has a definite place later in the lesson, it may be wise to begin the lesson with reports of completed assignments. The attention of the class can thus be directed to the significance and importance of self study, and pupils can be recognized for their efforts to learn.

AN IMAGINARY PROBLEM

The problems should be one which arises normally in the life of a class member. "What would you say if someone asked you why you go to church?" "What would you do if you were blamed for something you didn't do?" The problem needs to be such that it easily leads to the lesson.

USE OF VISUALS

A picture, map, object, filmstrip, or other instructional aid can be used effectively to create interest in the lesson.

Relating the Lesson

The following suggestions are effective ways to introduce a lesson:

RELATE IT TO PREVIOUS LESSONS

Each new lesson is part of the overall curriculum. It must be related to other lessons in order to interest the pupil and increase his understanding. Recent lessons should be carefully reviewed and the day's lesson associated with them. It also will help the pupil to know what place the lesson has in relation to the entire Bible.

Review procedures should be varied and fresh. A teacher does not lose time by reviewing previous teaching. More real progress can be made in thirty minutes after five minutes have been spent making a point of contact, than in thirty-five minutes effort to comprehend a disconnected lesson.

ANNOUNCE SUBJECT NATURALLY

A formal statement of the topic is not necessary, but an interesting, informative, perhaps surprise presentation may grow out of the review period. The announcement of the topic of the lesson should attract as much attention as the headlines of a newspaper.

STATE OBJECTIVES

Some teachers believe that it is wise to disclose their aims and objectives. Others insist that an application is more effective if the aim is not told in advance. Not all lessons need the same treatment. When there are temperance, missionary, or other special or seasonal lessons, the object of the lesson can easily be announced in advance.

MAKE THE OUTLINE CLEAR

Like the lead in a newspaper item, there is value in presenting a leading thought to stimulate interest in what is to follow. Sometimes an abbreviated, or even complete outline may be presented. However, if the teacher does not follow his outline, it is a mistake to reveal it.

DEVELOPING THE LESSON

"Well begun is half done." Having introduced the lesson, the teacher should proceed as he planned during his lesson preparation. The teaching of the lesson will reveal the quality of his preparation.

As the teacher presents the lesson, he must remember that he does not actually teach unless someone learns. The best test is not what the teacher says, but what his pupils learn.

Stimulate Thought

For this purpose the question may be most effective. The teacher who uses a series of thought-provoking inquiries will likely accomplish his purpose. Whenever information is imparted, the class should be expected to think it through with the teacher. Good teaching requires that the pupil be tested regularly to keep him alert and to see if he is profiting from the lesson.

One method of guiding thought is the pattern of deductive thinking. The teacher begins with a principle or general statement. This is followed by a number of illustrations. Then pupils are involved in seeking further examples from their own lives. The deductive method is like a cone.

The Point

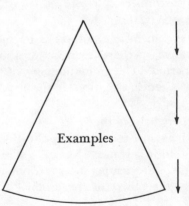

The Pupil's Experience[2]

Encourage Expression

It is important that every pupil be stimulated to think. He must also be encouraged to express his thoughts. What a person expresses, he is most likely to remember.

In addition to reproducing the facts of the lesson, the teacher should help the learner express himself by giving his own interpretation and his own understanding of the lesson. This best can be accomplished with inductive teaching. With this approach the teacher first enlists the help of the pupils in gathering pertinent facts or illustrations. As a result the class arrives at laws, or general principles, or the point. The knowledge and experiences of class members are used to reach the principle. The inverted cone illustrates this inductive approach.

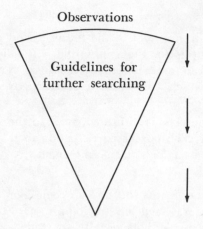

Observations

Guidelines for
further searching

The Point[3]

Apply Truth

The teacher should lead his class to face specific situations in which they need to practice the Christian ideal. This exercise will result in growth in grace. With constant emphasis on the application as well as the acquisition of knowledge, especially in the early years, pupils will learn and will make application of the lesson to their choice of conduct, course of action, attitudes, and overall spiritual life.

Because there is mental activity as well as physical, at times self-expression may take the form of self-restraint. Refusing to say or do what is wrong is nonetheless self-expression. Character is made up not only of impulses but also of restraints.

CLOSING THE LESSON

The lesson normally should not end abruptly. Careful consideration should be given to a fitting conclusion. The teacher should plan for three to five minutes of unhurried and prayerful application.

Summarize the Lesson

The teacher's presentation should include a summary of the lesson. Questions or class discussion may break into the planned outline, but the teacher should take time to sum up the results of the class period emphasizing the fundamental facts of the lesson. What are the important truths? What practical lessons have been taught? What final application should be made? How has Christ been revealed as the Savior of sinners? How can the lesson be demonstrated at home, at school, at work?

Anticipate Future Lessons

The closing minutes of the lesson period provide a good time to prepare pupils for the truths that will follow in successive lessons. They can experience a panoramic view of the days and weeks ahead which will stimulate eagerness by whetting their learning appetites.

Before the class is dismissed, refer to the next lesson and present plans for each pupil's participation in it. This is a good way to arouse interest and make assignments.

AROUSE INTEREST

The teacher wants the class to come back enthusiastically. By some startling statement or striking question, curiosity and interest can be aroused. Authors usually conclude a chapter so that the reader can hardly wait for the next chapter of a serial story. In the same manner, an expert teacher finishes the day's portion of "the most interesting story in the world," with such a climactic ending that the entire class will look forward to the next installment.

MAKE ASSIGNMENTS

Assignments must be carefully planned ahead of time, but the animated way in which they are assigned will determine the interest and enthusiasm of class members.

SUMMARY

Teaching is a skill which can be learned and improved. Most teachers can increase their effectiveness by carefully following planned procedures.

The teacher must utilize the initial class time to capture interest and attention. This begins when the first pupil arrives. During the introductory period of the lesson presentation, it is helpful to establish contact with the class in order to relate the lesson to their thinking.

The teacher will present his lesson according to the plan he has developed. In doing this he stimulates pupils to think, to express their thoughts, and to apply the lesson to their own lives. Both the inductive and deductive teaching approaches are fruitful procedures.

The lesson should end with an appropriate close. This includes a summary of materials presented as well as an introduction to future lessons.

NOTES

1. John T. Sisemore, *Blueprint for Teaching* (Nashville: Broadman Press, 1964), pp. 63-64.
2. Locke E. Bowman, Jr. *Straight Talks About Teaching in Today's Church* (Philadelphia: The Westminster Press, 1967), p. 38.
3. *Ibid.*, p. 39.

THINK

1. List two guiding principles for approaching the lesson period.
2. Specify five ways to arouse interest in the lesson.
3. Suggest steps to take in introducing a lesson.
4. Why is it helpful to relate the lesson to previous and following lessons?
5. How can a lesson be developed?
6. Compare the deductive and inductive approach to teaching.
7. How can the teacher lead his class to apply truth?
8. What is the value of calling class attention to future lessons?

TALK

1. Discuss teaching problems and their solutions related to one or more of the following topics:
   Arousing initial interest
   Involving the class in participation
   Making truths vital to the needs of the students
   Motivating students to prepare
2. Discuss the comparative values of the deductive and inductive approach to teaching.

ACT

1. Based on the principles stated in this course, have a fellow class member evaluate your teaching of a Sunday school class.
2. In outline form prepare two sets of teaching plans for a passage of Scripture using the deductive method for one and the inductive method for the other.

CHAPTER TEN

GOOD DISCIPLINE

Pupil self-discipline is the goal of discipline guidance.

God is the author of law and order; Satan is the author of confusion and chaos. The words *disciple* and *discipline* come from a word that means "trained in orderliness." For this reason Christians are admonished: "Let all things be done decently and in order."[1]

The Bible also teaches that children are to be brought up in the nurture and admonition of the Lord.[2] Nurture is instruction, but admonition is discipline. The teachers and officers in the church must not only impart instruction, but also exercise discipline. Pupils should learn to think. Moral and spiritual development requires that they also be trained in orderliness.

Disorder interferes with learning. Effective teaching is impossible when a class is out of control. Disorderly pupils nullify the teacher's efforts. Instead of practicing obedience, reverence, and the principles of Christian conduct, they learn disrespect for the teacher and disregard for God's house, God's Word, and God's day.

Children who are well behaved and obedient in other places may be disorderly in the church class. Why? Perhaps the teacher does not know how to express orderliness and Christian discipline. Perhaps he does not exercise authority. If the teacher lives a well-disciplined life, he will speak with the authority of God's Word. His manner and use of the Word of God will show authority and will bring effective results.

SETTING THE PATTERN

Order is contagious. So is disorder. One unruly pupil affects another; each distraction leads to another. A leader or teacher with a poorly prepared program invites trouble. An orderly atmosphere will command attention and respect. If chairs are properly arranged with songbooks in their places, the pupils likely will leave them that way. Books or papers on the floor extend an invitation for more to follow. An orderly atmosphere is conducive to orderly pupils. Teachers and officers should set a good example.

To stimulate good behavior, a teacher should check the classroom equipment and procedures. If there are discomforts, distractions, or disturbances, they should be corrected.

Discomforts

Classes should meet under favorable physical conditions. Pupils will not sit quietly if they are uncomfortable in chairs that are too large or too small. The result is wiggling, weariness, and unrest. Poor ventilation and extremes of temperature also contribute to discipline problems. Absence of coat racks can also prove to be a disturbing element. Pupils ought to be as comfortable in Bible classes as they are in their school classrooms.

Distractions

There are many distractions which make it difficult for a teacher to gain and hold attention. Separate classrooms help eliminate rivals which contend for the attention of pupils. Curtains afford partial privacy from visual distractions, but they do not obliterate sounds.

Disturbances

Some officers interrupt the lesson to distribute offering envelopes or literature or make announcements which may upset the teacher, the class, and the lesson. A superintendent should protect his teachers from disturbances so that they might have sufficient time and privacy for the lesson.

EXAMPLE OF THE TEACHER

The pupil's conduct will be affected by the example of his teacher. The teacher needs to recognize this fact and give special attention to his own physical, mental, and spiritual life.

Appearance

A teacher should dress carefully, avoiding extremes in clothes. Hair should be carefully groomed. The entire appearance should be neat and clean.

Striking mannerisms or peculiarities will draw attention from the lesson and be an indirect cause of disorder. The teaching rather than the teacher should occupy the pupil's thought. When this relative position is reversed, mental confusion follows.

Self-Control

Most teachers hope that God will transform their restlesss boys and girls into quiet, attentive pupils, but few teachers pray for their own self-mastery. The Holy Spirit-controlled teacher is victorious. Even the most extenuating circumstances should not cause the teacher to lose control of himself. He who does not control himself is not likely to control others. Many things may try his patience, and he needs to be on guard lest he become irritated and impatient.

Pupils quickly discover if the teacher is in a state of confusion. If he is, they will disregard his leadership. To be effective, the teacher must experience the "fruit of the Spirit" and demonstrate the grace that makes pleasant and cordial relationship between teacher and pupil. The calm, quiet, forceful mastery of our Lord impressed His listeners and made them listen to His words. In every controversy He was master of the situation.

Preparation

The teacher must be master of his subject if he is to influence his pupils. The lesson itself should keep order. The poorly-prepared teacher will have trouble. Orderliness in instruction leads to orderliness in conduct. Disorder leads to inattention and a lack of interest.

Self-Image

A pupil quickly perceives the teacher's image of himself. Every teacher needs to undertake some honest self-exploration. Discipline problems may be related to his own emotional stresses such as fatigue, a quarrel at home, or job insecurity. Sometimes the mischief of the child is resultant from the teacher's lack of experience. He may feel he is not cut out to be a teacher or that students know more than he does. When the teacher has resolved some of these questions, he will evidence confidence which will help students accept him.

ORDERLINESS OF THE PUPIL

Disorder may be caused by external conditions or be intentional action by a pupil. Some disorderly children simply may be thoughtless, restless, or unknowingly self-centered.

Thoughtlessness

The Christian teacher should know which pupils are thoughtless and which are intentionally disorderly. Pupils may be taught reverence for sacred things, but it may be difficult for them to carry out their best intentions.

Many churches provide systematic training in the early years of a child's life. They believe that reverence for sacred things can become a part of life. If proper conduct patterns are formed in the early departments, children will more likely be well behaved in subsequent departments.

Restlessness

Nervous tensions and frustrations are on the increase, even among Christians. Emotionally-disturbed children are not uncommon. The teacher must help these children, as well as the boys and girls who are naturally restless.

The average child is an active creature. He delights in doing something. If his teacher does not keep him involved, he will supply his own entertainment. These wide-awake pupils need a full program of activities that will give them opportunities to participate in the lesson. If good order is to be maintained, the active pupil will need a well-planned program of lesson materials and expressional activities.

Self-Centeredness

The self-centered child always wants his own way. He is the center of attention. His contribution seldom harmonizes with the lesson, and it is difficult for him to relate to the overall plan. He may be a discipline problem primarily in his disturbing relationships with other pupils.

Here is what one teacher did when an energetic pupil blew a whistle in class.

The teacher said, "Johnny has a whistle. A whistle is a good thing. What is a whistle good for?" Several replied. Then the application was skillfully made. The warnings and admonitions of the Bible were referred to as God's manner of attracting attention. The Bible says, "Blow the trumpet in Zion"—a whistle blown for God's people. The theme was developed helpfully. In the course of the diversion the teacher asked for the whistle, took it in her hand, commented on its construction, and assured Johnny she would return it after the completion of the lesson.

GUIDELINES FOR DISCIPLINE

Good discipline does not just happen. It results from specific preparation on the part of the teacher. The following teacher actions will help reduce discipline problems.

Understand the Nature and Purpose of Discipline

The quiet, controlled child and the undisturbed class are not necessarily the ideal toward which discipline should lead. Discipline looks beyond immediate emergency situations. There will always be those occasions where immediate action by the teacher is necessary. However, external control is only temporarily effective. The child needs help in the maturation process to develop a satisfactory image of himself, so he also will grow in inner control.

Lay a Foundation for Discipline

Discipline begins with the general atmosphere which the teacher establishes. Loving the pupils, exhibiting a spirit of warmth, meeting their needs in teaching, and developing personal strength through faith in God will set the stage for increasing discipline.

Early in the classroom experience pupils should become aware of the type of behavior which is expected. Guiding class members to see and accept the right behavior is the secret of good discipline.

Understand the Source of the Problem

There is a tendency to label a child as mischievous, rebellious, or malicious, when he does not measure up to standards of behavior. It is important to remember that children are by nature active and lacking in self-control. Many things they do may be normal behavior at their age.

Often the behavior of the child is a signal that there is a deeper, underlying problem. When a child bullies other children, shows off, or is destructive, he may be saying, "I have a problem, help me!" Serious mistakes can be made by teachers who do not sincerely endeavor to uncover the real problem.

Establish Positive Relationships

Many discipline problems can be resolved through a deep concern for the welfare of the child and a relationship of love and acceptance.

Authority or superior physical strength may curb unwanted actions but only temporarily. Another method is to provide the pupil with repetitive lectures about what he should or should not do. But the lectures often fall on deaf ears. The long-term result of negative action may be more rebellion. Positive relationships are needed.

The teacher must exhibit genuine respect for the pupil as an individual in his own right and evidence a deep desire to help him.

Clarify Rules of Behavior

Students can participate in establishing acceptable patterns of behavior in the classroom. Often they will be more stringent in their demands than teachers. Students also can be called upon to assist in enforcing behavior.

The teacher has the responsibility to help all members of the class know what is expected. Pupils should know when they may talk or walk around, that destruction of property is not allowed, and that all persons have equal rights and opportunities. Unknown rules contribute little to good discipline.

Work in Cooperation With the Home

Teachers and parents share responsibility in helping children become disciplined individuals. Usually, a discussion with the parents concerning an unruly child will be helpful, both for parents and teachers. Sometimes the cause of a problem can be discovered by visiting the child in his home. Discussions with parents should be private so that the child does not feel the adult world is joining forces against him.

Pray Faithfully For Each Member

The wise teacher will plan, work, teach, and pray that the grace of God will transform each pupil in his class. The problems, disciplines, and sacrifices will all be forgotten in the joy of watching pupils accept Christ and grow in grace.

SUMMARY

The concern for discipline is basic to all Christian education. The teacher's aim is to help every person mature toward Christlikeness. This includes the development of self-discipline and inner-directed behavior in keeping with Christian goals and values.

Various sources of discipline problems can be eliminated by giving attention to potential discomforts, distractions, and disturbances. But essentially, good discipline begins with the teacher. His appearance, self-control, instruction, and self-image will be perceived by the pupils who will respond in keeping with the pattern which has been established.

Teachers need to understand that discipline is more than enforced good behavior. It is the effort to help pupils develop inner control. A knowledge of the pupil both personally and generally, will help to identify the source of problems. Teachers should recognize normal behavior and also behavior which stems from a deeper, underlying problem.

Warm, accepting relationships with the class members will go far toward solving behavior problems. In addition, teachers need to recognize that they are not working alone, but rather with parents who share their concern for the growth of the child and with the Lord who is more interested in the best for each pupil than either parent or teacher.

NOTES

1. I Corinthians 14:40
2. Ephesians 6:4

THINK

1. What is discipline?
2. How is discipline related to moral and spiritual development?
3. In what ways do disorderly pupils interfere with the work of the Lord?
4. What factors lead to disorder in a classroom?
5. How can a teacher help create an atmosphere of order?
6. List five guidelines for effective discipline.
7. How can understanding the child aid in better discipline?
8. How can students help establish acceptable classroom behavior?

TALK

1. Discuss a specific current discipline problem in a church class. Describe pupil actions and seek to determine causes for these. Endeavor to secure group concensus on a workable solution.
2. After each group member has talked with several children of different age groups to learn their attitudes toward discipline, discuss the findings and their meaning for church education programs.

ACT

1. Evaluate objectively your own appearance and mannerisms when teaching. Consider any ways you might be contributing to disorder. You may want to ask someone to observe your teaching and assist you in evaluation. Prepare a list of ways you can improve.
2. Select the child or person in your class you least like. Endeavor to evidence real love and interest and observe any changes in his attitude toward you. Anecdotal records will help.

CHAPTER ELEVEN

APPLYING THE TRUTH

Applied truth results in spiritual growth.

A basic purpose of all Bible teaching is to effect change for good in the lives of pupils. The real test of teaching is not what a pupil hears, but what he becomes. Education includes both the acquisition of knowledge and its use. An educator teaches so that the pupil learns facts and applies them to his life.

IMPORTANCE OF APPLICATION

The Christian teacher is responsible to help shape the lives of his pupils. To do this, he teaches the Word of God. However, his task is not completed when he has imparted Bible knowledge. He must help his pupils develop godly character and maturity.

Character Building

The sincere teacher looks for response in the life of each pupil. When godliness is manifested, he knows that the Word of God has been effective and that the lessons have been learned.

It is impossible to separate Christian character from Christian living. As character develops, it is expressed in living. The outward Christian life is the result of the Christ-formed character within. When Christ is acknowledged as Lord, the learner will be mastered by God's truth and will establish habits of study, prayer, reverence, worship, obedience, and unselfishness. An urgent desire to cultivate these habits should motivate the Christian teacher.

Christian Growth

Christian character grows by expression—not through dreaming or wishing or talking. The habit of doing nothing is as devastating as the habit of doing wrong. If instruction and inspiration are not expressed in action, they will destroy spiritual sensitivity and make response to the Holy Spirit's leading extremely difficult. Expressional activities must be incorporated in the teaching program, so that positive, active Christian character will be encouraged.

Christ's teaching methods included a strong emphasis on application. In the Sermon on the Mount He said, "Whosoever heareth these sayings of mine, and doeth them, I will liken him unto a wise man, which built his house upon a rock."[1] "Not every one that saith unto me, Lord, Lord, shall enter into the kingdom of heaven; but he that doeth the will of my Father which is in heaven."[2] "By their fruits ye shall know them."[3] He taught His disciples that the inner spiritual condition is manifested by outward deeds and actions. They did not learn this truth in a formal schoolroom. They shared His life and work. They lived as He lived. They learned right attitudes toward God and their fellow men. They sensed His motives and ministry. Then He sent them out to complete their training by practical experience in everyday life.

People develop Christian behavior patterns in the same way today. They learn to pray, not by defining or describing prayer, but by entering actively into prayer. They learn how to study God's Word by actual use of the Bible. They become reverent, obedient, unselfish by practicing these virtues.

Spiritual Foundation

The Word of God provides the foundation for Christian life and living. It is useless to attempt to build Christian character independent of instruction in it. The Bible is changeless in every changing age. It is "profitable for doctrine, for reproof, for correction, for instruction in righteousness."[4] The human "heart is deceitful above all things, and desperately wicked."[5] Pupils cannot build Christian faith on the foundation of everyday human experiences. The Bible is the chart and compass.

The Bible deals with life by recognizing sin and supplying God's remedy. It touches every inner and outer area—sports, social activities, home, school, church. The Bible meets life's greatest needs. Bible-centered lessons aimed at life-centered needs provide the most effective curriculums.

Our Lord laid great stress on application based on the Word of God. When He went into the synagogue at Nazareth, He read and expounded the first two verses of Isaiah 61.[6] His exposition provided an up-to-date application. He said that the words of this ancient prophet were fulfilled that very day. Years later, after His resurrection, when He met the disappointed disciples on the road to Emmaus, He drew from them the reason for their perplexity. He met their real life situation and comforted the sorrowful disciples by "expound[ing] unto them in all the scriptures the things concerning himself."[7] This was His method of Bible teaching. It was applied instruction. It was aimed at human need.

THE TEACHER'S EXAMPLE

The Spirit of God applies the truths of the Word to pupils' lives. However, the Spirit often uses the teacher to clarify the meaning of a lesson both by example and attitude.

Actions

No teacher can successfully relate truth until he has applied it to his own life. Pupils must constantly see exemplified in their teacher the biblical truth he wishes them to apply to their lives. This is a categorical imperative in Christian teaching. If pupils are to learn of Christ, teachers must be sure they themselves know Him and live as He would have them live.

The Lord Jesus accompanied His teaching by a constant demonstration of the truth. He exemplified meekness by girding Himself and washing the disciples' feet.[8] He frequently taught forgiveness,[9] but it was in His look of forgiveness, that Peter learned its real meaning after he had denied His Lord.[10]

Christ demonstrated forgiveness on the cross when He prayed, "Father, forgive them; for they know not what they do."[11] And even the hardened centurion acknowledged that Jesus was a righteous man.[12] Christ taught about prayer, but His disciples failed to understand until "it came to pass, that, as he was praying in a certain place, when he ceased, one of his disciples said unto him, Lord, teach us to pray, as John also taught his disciples."[13]

Attitudes

Truth is shared through relationships as well as transmitted by words. A recent study demonstrates that the attitude of junior high students toward God is not dependent on the amount of their Bible knowledge. Their attitudes are dependent on the attitudes of their parents toward God.[14] Teachers also transmit attitudes through frequent relationships with pupils. Often teachers will be more influential in the lives of their students by the attitudes they evidence than by what they say.

Many young people have testified that while they forgot the verbal instruction received in their youth, they could never forget the exemplary life of a godly teacher. The teacher's daily life must demonstrate his instruction in order to impress the hearts and minds of his pupils. Truths that have not helped the teacher will not help the class. The lesson must affect the teacher before it can bless the class.

The teacher can examine himself by asking: What has this lesson taught me? Am I better qualified for my work because I have studied this lesson? Do I exemplify the truth I am teaching to my class? This is the crucial part of a teacher's preparation.

PLANNING FOR APPLICATION

The application of the lesson is vitally related to the teacher's aim. In lesson preparation the teacher should plan to meet the specific needs of his pupils, both as a group and as individuals. In order to do this, careful plans must be made to personalize the lesson, relate it to life, and involve pupils in applying it to their own experiences.

Personalize Lesson

Application is based on pupil understanding and comprehension of biblical truth and then personally relating to it. The teacher leads the learners to discover the application for themselves. Among specific procedures which help personalize are:

Ask probing questions.

Confront the class with alternatives.

Lead them into actual or imaginative predicaments that require the application of the truth.

Focus attention on sub-Christian attitudes and activities.

Allow the members to express doubt, wonder, skepticism, and curiosity about points of application.

Help the members interpret their own experiences.[15]

Relate to Life

Until early adolescence, pupils have a limited power of generalization. They do not readily see the underlying principles of biblical teachings which apply to many different situations. Therefore, the teacher has to lead them to see these relationships. However, the teacher cannot force change upon those he teaches. They must be confronted with the Word and see its relationship to their own need, before they are ready to make a personal response.

Involve Pupils

Learning will be more effective when pupils participate in making the application. Sometimes the entire class can agree to select a certain behavior pattern, an attitude, or an activity which reflects the emphasis of the lesson. They may agree to follow this behavior pattern or set of values during the coming week. This can be followed by an evaluation of results in the review of the lesson the following week.

EMPHASES OF APPLICATION

There are several areas of spiritual development in which application of lesson content should be evident.

Salvation

It is imperative that every pupil understand his personal responsibility for a decision for Christ. Instruction should train him in the truths and procedures that will prepare for personal acceptance of Jesus Christ as Savior and Lord.

Spirituality

After conversion, the pupil should be given opportunities to grow spiritually. Regular attendance at church activities should result in systematic Bible study and prayer. Other helps to growth in grace are worship, singing, and Christian fellowship.

The aim of spirituality is the mature person in Christ. "Till we all come in the unity of the faith, and of the knowledge of the Son of God, unto a perfect man, unto the measure of the stature of the fulness of Christ."[16] As the reality of Christ increases by faith, the fruit of the Spirit[17] will also become more evident.

The Sunday school should provide training in worship. Individuals or classes can plan and lead the assembly. This will involve a study of the elements of worship, a search of the Scripture for the acts involved in worship, and an observation of the worship program of the church. It will require an evaluation of the prayers, hymns, devotional books, and periodicals that will help all participants understand and appreciate the experiences of worship.

Stewardship

The development of spiritual life also involves the pupil's personal responsibility for his use of time, abilities, and possessions. He should be taught to support the entire program of the church and to contribute his own money. The actual sharing of possessions provides the best learning. Even if his parents provide his offerings, the pupil should be taught true stewardship. To the degree the spirit of sacrificial sharing permeates the entire church, pupils will learn and practice stewardship of time, talents, and possessions.

Each generation needs training to be liberal, systematic, cheerful givers. Pupils need information about the object of their gifts as well as why they give. This will encourage them to practice Christian stewardship.

Service

An adequate curriculum, properly taught, should lead the pupil to a personal responsibility for his talents. The wise teacher knows how to capture every opportunity to direct pupils to worthwhile activities. He makes his instruction a laboratory course in Christian service as a stimulus for lifetime surrender to Christ in the home, in the church, in the community, in the world.

Christians need to live for Christ in their own homes. Children as well as adults should realize their responsibility for happiness at home. They should be encouraged to participate in the care of the home, and warned against shirking their duty. The entire family should share in the hospitality which the home extends to friends and neighbors, and take pride in demonstrating its attractiveness.

Each pupil also should be impressed with his responsibility to the church, especially if he is a member. This implies regular attendance, systematic contributions to its support, and active participation in its program. Pupils should be encouraged to secure new members and visit those who attend irregularly or drop out entirely.

In a wide-awake church organization there are many other service opportunities for members of all ages. Service can be rendered in the distribution of supplies or decoration of rooms for special occasions. Older students can help build up enrollment with a community survey or census.

There are additional opportunities in every community to minister to the needy, the sick, the lonely through a well-rounded program for children, young people, and adults. Civic and community enterprises also provide valuable opportunities for practical outreach.

Service should reach to people in other lands as well. Letters, missionary boxes, and gifts of money can express genuine and intelligent interest in the lives of others. Pupils must be brought to see their responsibility for evangelizing the entire world. They should be urged to obey Christ's commission, "Go ye therefore, and teach all nations . . . Teaching them to observe all things whatsoever I have commanded you . . . ."[18]

SUMMARY

The final test of all teaching is in the changed life of the pupil. This requires application of the truth for applying the truth builds character and provides for Christian growth and a spiritual foundation.

Much learning takes place through relationships. Pupils learn from what teachers are. Knowledge can be transmitted by an effective teaching process; however, life changes take place when the action and attitudes of the teacher corroborate his words.

Successful translation of truth into life requires deliberate planning on the part of the teacher. He must constantly strive to personalize biblical truth, relate it to the life situations which pupils are facing, and then involve them in action. The evidences of successful application are salvation, spirituality, stewardship, and service.

NOTES

1. Matthew 7:24
2. Matthew 7:21
3. Matthew 7:20
4. II Timothy 3:16
5. Jeremiah 17:9
6. Luke 4:16-21
7. Luke 24:27
8. John 13:14
9. Matthew 6:15; 18:21, 22
10. Luke 22:61, 62
11. Luke 23:34
12. Luke 23:47
13. Luke 11:1
14. Lawrence O. Richards, "The Idea Bank," *United Evangelical Action* (Spring 1971), pp. 7, 9.
15. John T. Sisemore, *Blueprint for Teaching* (Nashville: Broadman Press, 1964), p. 88.
16. Ephesians 4:13
17. Galatians 5:22, 23
18. Matthew 28:19, 20

THINK

1. What did Christ say about the relationship of knowledge and actions?
2. How can the Christian teacher help his pupils form Christian habits?
3. Why must lesson applications be based on the Word of God?
4. Illustrate how Christ accompanied His teaching by demonstration of truth.
5. Why must the Sunday school teacher first apply Bible truth to his own life?
6. List three steps in planning for application.
7. How can the class be involved in carrying the lesson into life?
8. List four general areas of student need that the teacher should plan to meet in lesson application.

TALK

1. It has been said, "The real test of teaching is what a pupil becomes." Discuss the validity of this statement using illustrations from life situations about which you know.
2. Discuss how advertisers endeavor to apply their message whether written or spoken. Consider both direct and more subtle application and whether teachers should be similar salesmen.

ACT

1. Examine several Sunday school manuals for one or more departments in which you are interested to see how the authors apply lesson truth to life situations. Give an additional application for each lesson in at least one manual.
2. After tracing the teaching ministry of Jesus in one of the gospels, discuss times when Jesus' teaching was immediately applied and times when the application took place later.

CHAPTER TWELVE

TESTING THE TEACHING

Testing evaluates both pupil learning and the instructor's teaching.

Evaluation of teaching is important. Most teachers are surprised to discover how little knowledge is actually retained by their pupils. Because of this there is a vital need to evaluate teaching methods and emphases and to review lessons.

A Bible test was given to 81 sophomores and juniors in high school—nearly all were regular Sunday school attendants. The questions were purely factual. Who was the first man? Name the Pentateuch. Who led the children of Israel from Egypt? Who was the first king of Israel? Who wrote most of the Psalms? Name the four Gospels. Name four of Paul's epistles. The average grade was 35%.[1]

Sooner or later every teacher's effectiveness will be judged, not only by men, but also by God. I Corinthians 3:1-15 indicates that those who teach cannot escape the testing of their work and workmanship.

If teaching is careless, superficial, blundering, the results will be reflected in the failure of our pupils to grasp the truths they should learn, and in the consequent impoverishment of their lives. If our teaching is earnest, thoughtful, skillful, the results will be manifest in the growth and development of our pupils as they incorporate the truths of Christianity in their character and conduct.[2]

Testing a pupil's knowledge is as possible as teaching him the truth. Often, those who test their pupils find that a major difficulty is the inadequacy of their own teaching. If a testing program is planned, it is important that the teacher impress the pupils at the time of class presentation with the facts he wishes them to remember.

ORAL TESTING

Much of the testing can be done by means of a well-conducted oral recitation. This should be more than a mere repetition of exact words or phrases. By testing knowledge, we "put it on trial." We submit pupil understanding to cross-examination to determine whether it is clear or confused. Pupils should be encouraged to say in their own way what they understand to be the truth. If the teacher is to obtain a true picture of pupil understanding, the test should be thorough, searching, correct, and inspiring.

The teacher also must be alert to attitudes and knowledge as expressed by these responses. Often a pupil's misunderstanding of one word or phrase will break communication and the teacher should not proceed until it has been explained.

Oral testing requires pupil preparation and wise teacher conduct of the test.

Pupil Preparation

While it is difficult to get Sunday school pupils to study at home, they will if two principles are followed. The teacher must expect pupil cooperation and must recognize pupil preparation.

If oral testing is to be effective, sufficient time should be spent in preparing for it. Carefully assigned preparation leads to a willing, intelligent response from the class. If pupils are expected to study at home, they need guidance, assistance, and a clear understanding of what they are expected to know. Sources for securing the needed information also should be provided.

Teacher Conduct of Test

A wise teacher does not indicate in advance which pupil is to be called on to recite or in what order pupils will be selected. He may call on the same person twice in succession in order to keep the class alert. Such uncertainty requires each pupil to follow closely the response of all others. The assignment is never made until the question has been asked or the topic stated. No one is overlooked nor is one person called on too frequently.

The "concert" method or the "consecutive" method for recitation seldom works. In the former, a few prepared pupils will lead the answers and the others will join in. In the latter, the only pupils who give close attention are those who are reciting or expecting to be called upon next.

Assuming there has been home preparation and previous study, there are two methods which are widely used for oral testing.

QUESTION METHOD

By the wise use of questions, the teacher will unfold the subject systematically and logically. Questions should not be stereotype. They will, to a large extent, be prompted by the previous responses of pupils. This provides freshness and spontaneity.

TOPICAL METHOD

The topical method compels the pupil to state his opinions. It makes him responsible for organizing his own thoughts and expressing them. Skillful teacher guidance will keep the class from being diverted into unrelated discussions. Combining the question and the topical methods will test what the pupil knows and provide him with an opportunity to support his opinion.

WRITTEN EXAMINATIONS

Schools and colleges often give written examinations. The work of a term, a semester, or even a year, is subject to a general review and examination. Bible knowledge should be obtained and tested by the same methods used in other teaching areas.

The Bible teaches that children should be brought up "in the nurture and admonition of the Lord."[3] Nurture involves knowledge. Admonition refers to behavior. Both knowledge and behavior should be examined.

Many people relate examinations to wearisome, last-minute cramming, or the painful experience of trying to put on paper what has been laboriously or hurriedly memorized. They are concerned about unanticipated questions and unanswerable problems. The result is that church teachers and pupils alike have avoided testing in general. Yet, if teaching is taken seriously, and is earnest, thoughtful, and skillful, various methods of testing can be used. A well-designed examination challenges the pupil to rethink what he has learned and to express his learning in a life-related context.

Teachers also may require the preparation of a paper, or report to show research work. This independent study has genuine educational value.

BIBLE KNOWLEDGE TESTS

The teacher is closely involved in Bible testing. He prepares the questions and judges the answers. He may assign topics and evaluate the response. Often the use of a pretest or carefully planned discussion before beginning a series of Bible lessons will reveal what should be emphasized in class and provide a basis for comparison when an examination is given. The teacher who understands modern testing procedures knows that they can be interesting, stimulating, and extremely profitable. If corrected immediately they also can be a learning experience.

Areas of Tests

Pupils should be tested in at least three areas of Bible knowledge.

HISTORICAL

There are many historical facts in the Bible narrative. These should be studied chronologically. For examination purposes, the facts may be jumbled and the pupil asked to rearrange them in logical order until they are impressed upon his mind.

BIOGRAPHICAL

The pupils may be asked to identify Bible characters, arrange the names in chronological order, or supply missing information or events.

GEOGRAPHICAL

On an outline map pupils can locate the cities, sections, and countries where important biblical events took place. Small maps may be reproduced, purchased, or drawn by the pupils. It is important that all pupils be familiar with the geographical factors connected with their Bible study.

Types of Tests

Many types of tests have been used successfully in general education. The same types have been adapted for use in Sunday school. Often the publishers of curriculum material include suggested tests in pupils' and teachers' manuals. There are at least four types of tests with which pupils are familiar.

TRUE—FALSE

In this type of test the pupil reads a series of statements. Some are true, some false. The pupil evaluates and circles the correct answer. The following test is based on Luke 2:47-52.

The wise doctors in the temple were surprised at the wisdom shown in Jesus' answers.	T	F
He asked Mary and Joseph, "How is it that ye sought me?"	T	F
Jesus said He had to be about His Father's business.	T	F
Mary and Joseph did not understand what He told them.	T	F
The doctors said, "Stay with us."	T	F
Jesus stayed in Jerusalem at the Temple after Mary and Joseph found Him.	T	F
Jesus went home with His parents to Nazareth.	T	F
Jesus was obedient to (subject unto) His parents.	T	F
His mother forgot all about what had happened.	T	F
Jesus kept growing in wisdom and stature, and in favor with God and man.	T	F

COMPLETION

Completion tests are more exacting than true-false tests. In the true-false test there is a 50% chance of guessing right. In completion tests, the pupil fills in the information indicated by blank spaces. The following example illustrates what might be done after studying II Kings 20.

Hezekiah was sick unto ....
The prophet who came to see Hezekiah was ....
The prophet told Hezekiah that he was going to ....
Hezekiah sadly turned his face to ....
Hezekiah prayed that God would remember he had walked in ....
As Hezekiah prayed, he ....

MULTIPLE CHOICE

Multiple choice tests offer a fine opportunity to discover a pupil's knowledge. Here is a sample geographical test. The pupil underscores the name of the correct answer.

Village that didn't see many mighty works because of unbelief.
Jerusalem, Nazareth, Capernaum, Bethsaida.
Province through which the Jews hated to pass.
Berea, Judea, Galilee, Samaria.
Village where Jesus was always welcome.
Bethany, Nazareth, Gergesa, Jericho.
Body of water that obeyed Jesus' command.
Great Sea, Dead Sea, Sea of Galilee, Jordan River.
Region that had a revival because a man told what Jesus did for him.
Syria, Decapolis, Caesarea Philippi, Wilderness.

MATCHING

The matching test is usually popular with pupils. It requires nothing more than the use of lines or numbers. In the following example, the pupil is told that the book of Philemon contains the names and identifying statements of eleven persons. He is asked to match these by drawing a line from the name to the correct statement.

The "brother" whose greeting Paul sent	Paul
Runaway slave	Timothy
Philemon's wife	Philemon
Philemon's son	Onesimus
A great missionary in prison	Apphia
A rich man of Colosse	Archippus
A fellow-prisoner of Paul	Epaphras
Paul's fellow-laborers	Mark, Aristarchus, Demas, Luke

BEHAVIORAL TESTS

The tests just studied are used to determine the pupil's

knowledge of Bible content. Churches also desire to measure spiritual growth and behavior. This is more difficult because life consists largely of habits of thinking, feeling, or acting that have become deeply rooted through repetition. Children need assistance in the formation of right habits. Church teachers and parents should cooperate in this important ministry. Jesus emphasized this phase of Christian instruction when He said, "Whosoever heareth these sayings of mine, and doeth them, I will liken him unto a wise man, which built his house upon a rock."[4] Among several ways to measure behavior are the use of records and self-rating scales.

Records

Successful church schools are not satisfied with mere records of attendance. Several excellent systems have been developed to record additional information, including the interest and response of pupils. These systems tabulate such items as lesson preparation, church attendance, family background, punctuality, use of Bible, prayer life, soul winning, enlisting new pupils, and offering.

Although these records do not measure results in the life of the pupil, they do indicate some areas that contribute to Christian character.

Self-Rating Scales

After a pupil has accepted the Lord Jesus Christ, it is essential that he be shown how to relate his faith and his works. "Even so faith, if it hath not works, is dead, being alone."[5]

The supreme achievement of Christian education is well-rounded Christian character. By Christian character we mean that habits, knowledge, attitudes, choices, and conduct are organized around Christ as the center, so that all life is under His control. The attainment of this ideal is not instantaneous but progressive. Progress toward it is to be measured by character tests.

Self-rating scales are popular and useful in helping one discover one's strong and weak points. Just as one looks in a mirror to check upon personal appearance, so one might profitably use a series of questions to determine inner qualities of character.[6]

Self-rating scales also are useful in evaluating pupil behavior. Two types of scales can be used. One provides self-evaluation in terms of the frequency of an action: always, usually, sometimes, seldom, never.

	Always	Usually	Sometimes	Seldom	Never
Providing help for a person in trouble					

Another permits evaluation in terms of a scale and the pupil is asked to evaluate his behavior on a scale of 1 to 10, where 10 is the highest score.

Obedience to parents (circle the appropriate number)

1   2   3   4   5   6   7   8   9   10

A class can identify a number of Christian behavior patterns based on the lesson. On this basis a simple test can be constructed. This provides a significant tool for testing behavior.

Pupils should be encouraged to check their own Christian lives. They should be taught to be both honest and objective.

ATTITUDE AND CHOICE

Church teaching should lead to the formation of Christian attitudes and choices. It is necessary to test these outcomes, but it is not easy to measure progress in spiritual realms. Regeneration and spiritual growth are produced by the Holy Spirit. Who can fathom His mysterious operations or know the time when conviction is brought to the heart? The teacher must be sensitive to the moods of the class. He must know how to take advantage of that moment when the Holy Spirit reveals that the time for decision has come. Under God, the consecrated, discerning teacher will have the joy of leading his pupils to the saving knowledge of the Lord Jesus Christ. He may also lead them to the surrender of their lives to the perfect will of God. This is the ultimate aim and test of Bible-centered, Christ-honoring teaching.

SUMMARY

Studies repeatedly indicate that many Sunday school pupils possess only minimal Bible knowledge. Although church schools have avoided the use of testing programs, responsible teaching includes an evaluation of results. These results are not limited to Bible knowledge, but extend to attitudes and behavior.

A simple approach to determine pupil knowledge is the use of the recitation method. Through the skillful employment of questions, pupils are given the opportunity to share their knowledge, insights, convictions, and decisions. It also is possible for teachers to develop and utilize various forms of Bible tests. True-false, completion, multiple choice, and matching tests are most popular.

Behavioral tests are more difficult to construct. Weekly records give an indication of participation in church-related activities. Self-rating scales are useful in helping pupils take a careful look at their own lives in terms of principles that are based on the biblical passages they have studied.

NOTES

1. Gaines S. Dobbins, *The Improvement of Teaching in the Sunday School* (Nashville: Broadman Press, 1955), p. 153.
2. *Ibid.*, p. 150.
3. Ephesians 6:4
4. Matthew 7:24
5. James 2:17
6. Dobbins, pp. 161, 162.

THINK

1. Why is testing an important part of Bible teaching?
2. How can class recitation be utilized for testing purposes?
3. What is the possible place of the essay in Bible testing?
4. In what areas of Bible knowledge should the pupil be tested?
5. Describe the merits of each of four types of Bible tests.
6. Why is it important to test behavior?
7. What is the unique value to pupils of a self-rating test?
8. What is the ultimate test of Bible-centered teaching?

TALK

1. Discuss possible ways to enlist the cooperation of pupils in a program of testing them about biblical truths they were taught.
2. Discuss various probable responses, at different age levels, to the same problematic life situation. Show how the measure of spiritual development is indicated by these responses.

ACT

1. Investigate Christian education testing programs for helpful data concerning methods and results of testing. It may be necessary to contact several denominational and interdenominational groups.
2. Identify a number of Christian behavior patterns presented in a lesson taught in your church school. With the use of a self-rating scale, construct a test of behavior which can be used before and after the lesson to indicate the need for the lesson and any changes which occur.

Since 1930 Evangelical Teacher Training Association has been used of God to strengthen and advance evangelical Christian education. E.T.T.A. leadership preparation materials are planned to preserve and propagate the rich gospel *message* through good educational *methods*.

Christian education is presented as an important factor in the fulfillment of Christ's commission "Go ye therefore, and *teach* all nations . . . *teaching* them to observe all things, whatsoever I have commanded you" (Matt. 28:19, 20). In order to minister broadly in the advancement of Christian education, E.T.T.A. functions on three educational levels, each of which complements the others.

The PRELIMINARY CERTIFICATE PROGRAM is designed for local church and community leadership training classes. Six vital and challenging subjects are covered. The three Bible survey courses are *Old Testament Survey—Law and History, Old Testament Survey—Poetry and Prophecy, New Testament Survey*. Christian education required courses include *Understanding People, Understanding Teaching* or *Teaching Techniques, Sunday School Success*.

An Award Credit Card is issued for satisfactory work in each course that is taught by an instructor approved by E.T.T.A. The Preliminary Teachers Certificate is granted when the required six courses have been completed.

The ADVANCED CERTIFICATE PROGRAM is taught in E.T.T.A.-affiliated Bible institutes* and in local church and community classes. The program consists of a minimum of twelve courses, twelve lessons each, and leads to the Advanced Teachers Certificate. It includes the six courses of the Preliminary Certificate Program and the following six courses: *The Missionary Enterprise, Evangelize Thru Christian Education, The Triune God, Biblical Beliefs, Church Educational Ministries* or *Vacation Bible School, Your Bible*.

The HIGHER EDUCATION PROGRAM provides specific preparation for training leadership. A Silver Seal Advanced Teachers Certificate is awarded by Associate member schools of E.T.T.A.* This Certificate qualifies the recipient to teach all preliminary courses leading to E.T.T.A. credit. Institutions of higher education which hold Active membership in E.T.T.A.* offer extensive Bible study as well as a wide selection of courses in Christian education and related subjects. A Diploma is awarded in recognition of required educational attainment and qualifies the holder to conduct the E.T.T.A. leadership preparation program in church or community classes.

*A list of member schools is available on request.